T0197146

HOW TO RECOGNIZE HEAVENLY SIGNS FROM OUR BELOVED PETS

STEVEN H. WOODWARD

authorHOUSE®

AuthorHouse™
1663 Liberty Drive
Bloomington, IN 47403
www.authorhouse.com
Phone: 833-262-8899

Published by AuthorHouse 12/05/2022

ISBN: 978-1-6655-7749-6 (sc)
ISBN: 978-1-6655-7747-2 (hc)
ISBN: 978-1-6655-7748-9 (e)

Library of Congress Control Number: 2022922502

Print information available on the last page.

This book is printed on acid-free paper.

TABLE OF CONTENTS

DEDICATION

I dedicate this book to God and also to my little dog BJ that God sent to me that began my journey into the Amazing Afterlife.

And to my wife, sons, and grandchildren who have a great love of animals.

Also to Jasper, Petey, Duke, and all the animals whose spirits I have bonded with in my life.

And a big thanks to all my readers, supporters, and to all rescuers and shelter workers.

God bless you all.

S.H.W.

*"Therefore I say unto you,
What things soever ye desire, when ye pray,
believe that ye receive them,
and ye shall have them." (Mark 11:24)*

PROLOGUE

*"Animals are a joy to the soul,
and they make the spirit whole."*
-Steven H. Woodward

This book was written to help pet lovers recognize all the signs that our beloved pets send to us from heaven. And also to prove that these *Signs, Dreams, Visions, and Spiritual Visitations* from our beloved animals are real. I will show that it has been proven through scientific facts and biblical scriptures that our beloved animals are able to communicate with us and that they can and do visit us from the afterlife through spiritual communication. These spiritual signs have been happening for centuries and continue to this day. Most of the patriarchs in the bible experienced many types of spiritual phenomena, and some of them experienced it more than once.

God has sent angels, human and animal spirits to help those in need and to give signs to those who ask. Sometimes Jesus would show up in spirit to help or to communicate information to the prophets. And many times he gave them a divine job to do. There were also many other people in the bible that were given signs, dreams, and visions such as kings, pharaohs, and other gentiles. After reading this book you will know why and how our animals can *send us signs from the afterlife.* And you will be able to know and recognize these signs that our beloved animals send to us from the afterlife. After reading this book you will have no doubts that your beloved animal is in heaven and is able to contact you through some type of spiritual communication.

Some people think that visions, dreams, signs, and spiritual visitations are evil and from the devil, but this is not true. If one prays to God for these things it is not evil or from the devil. If people say that God does not do these things then they should study their bible more carefully because the bible is full of visions, dreams, and signs from the spirit realm. And this includes spiritual visitations from God, Jesus, angels, humans, and *animals.* The bible also tells us that the spirit of your deceased animal can communicate with you if you ask God. And you will see that God *wants* us to ask him for these spiritual things. But it is important for you to know that you must ask Jesus for these things. Anything else may be dangerous and you could possibly invite evil into your life.

Dreams, visions, signs, and spiritual visitations are God-given and they help us to grow closer to God and become more spiritual. Millions of people have had these spiritual experiences and many are very credible people such as doctors, lawyers, military personnel, prophets, and even famous people. And not to mention everyday people too. Are we to ignore all of these witnesses? When there are that many credible people saying they have had a divine experience, there is something to it. Some years ago I did not believe this to be possible, but I know these things are real because I have had visions and been given signs myself.

There are also people who have had NDE's (near death experiences) which are spiritual experiences that occur while a person is clinically dead for a short period of time. And these people have given undeniable proof of the afterlife and of the spirit world through *Vertical* NDE's. We will discuss this type of NDE in chapter six and how it proves that NDE's are true divine experiences.

Once you have had a divine experience you know in your heart that it is true and you won't care whether anyone believes it or not. I have divided these spiritual phenomena into five classes of spiritual *contact*:

1. *Feelings:* While awake: This is a type of knowing through (spiritual) feeling. Like feeling the spirit of your beloved pet in the room with you. You are basically feeling the frequency of your beloved pet's spirit. This also includes a premonition of something to come, or something that will happen.
2. *Audible:* While awake: You hear an audible sound such as a bark, meow, tags jingling, paws on the floor, etc.

3. *Optical:* While awake: Observing a spiritual manifestation. This is where you may see a spiritual manifestation of your animal, although it may be only for an instant. This includes any other type of visual sign.
4. *Actual Contact:* While awake or asleep: This is where you feel the spirit of your deceased pet touch you somewhere on your body, in some form or fashion. Perhaps a snuggle, a kiss, or you may feel something brush up against you.
5. *NDE/Vision/Dream:* While awake, asleep, or deceased: An open-trance vision occurs through deep prayer while awake. A divine dream happens while asleep. An NDE occurs while deceased for a short period of time. In these three events your spirit *is taken to heaven.* There you will see loved ones, which includes your beloved pets. You are able to talk (thought communication), hear, and touch the spirits of your beloved animals in heaven. And of course, one will see Jesus.

The bible is full of divine afterlife signs, visions, dreams, and spiritual visitations from the book of Genesis to the book of Revelation.

*"In order to love,
one must possess a soul.
Animals know more about
unconditional love than humans do.
So therefore animals must have souls."*
-Steven H. Woodward

CHAPTER ONE

COMMUNICATING WITH ANIMALS FROM THE AFTERLIFE AND THE SPIRIT FREQUENCIES

"Every animal knows more than you do."
-Nez Perce Proverb

Animals communicate with us and to other animals in many earthly forms. We hear the various vocal sounds house-hold pets make such as barking, whining, purring, meowing, etc. Animal lovers know that they can talk to their animal and they understand them. Many animals respond to certain words that we teach them such as, "no, sit, and come here" along with many other commands. Think of military and police K-9 dogs that have been trained for combat. And also service dogs that are trained to help people with disabilities.

These animals are trained using various methods of communications. And they know and understand these vocal commands.

The eyes can communicate many things and there are also many other ways of communicating without speaking both here on earth, and also from the afterlife. All animal lovers know that their pet can express thoughts to their owner through their eyes, vocal sounds, body movements, and facial expressions. In order to be able to communicate you must have a soul. And animals do have souls/spirits. Not only do animals communicate with us here on earth but they also communicate to us from the afterlife. Let's examine the many various ways to communicate that will give us an idea of the myriad of different ways to communicate both here and into the afterlife; be it the visible or the *invisible*. First, let's look at earthly communication from our pets and then we will look at the spiritual communications that they send to us from the afterlife.

Many animals use their eyes and other body parts to communicate the same as we do. Household pets such as cats and dogs use their eyes, tales, paws, body language, and vocal sounds to communicate. Squirrels use their tales to communicate, as do other animals. Birds and many other animals use sounds, songs, and dancing in order to communicate. A peacock will spread its tail feathers (called a train) to attract females. Just because we may not understand an animal's communication through their particular body movements or their auditory sounds, doesn't mean that that particular animal is not communicating to us or to another animal. It means we just don't understand their language. Animals communicate all the time here on earth and from the spiritual realm. You see, earthly communication from animals can be misunderstood and not recognizable as with spiritual communication. We must understand and know the signs of spiritual communication when we see or hear it. There are also spiritual communications that we and animals use here on earth as seen below in the next few paragraphs.

I had a black and white Boston Terrier and his name was Petey. We hung bells on the doorknob inside of our back door so we could hear if anyone uninvited tried to come in the door. Petey learned that if he stood up and took his paw and hit the bells we would know to come and let him outside to do his business. We did not teach him this. He figured this out himself. He was communicating to us through the sound of the bells.

Three main ways of communicating with your animal are: observing, listening, and talking. We observe their eyes, body language, and facial expressions. Sometimes even a simple look sends a message. When my wife gives me that certain look I know to run and hide. I know without her saying anything, that she is not pleased with me. This is a form of *spiritual communication* and it does not require speech.

Observation is a form of communication. I can watch someone do something and then I can do it. Animals can learn and communicate through observation too. For example, if I want to train my dog Jasper to perform tricks I will use my hands, arms, voice, and fingers. I will show him what I want him to do and he will respond. Example: We purchased a treat bowl which is a bowl with a snap-on top. The bowl is filled up with small treats and it has two small holes on the bottom edges where the treats fall out when rocked. It has to be smacked and knocked around so it will rock and allow the treats to spill out of the holes. I showed Jasper that if I hit it with my hand it rocked and treats came out. Jasper watched me and after about five minutes he was smacking it across the room gobbling up the little treats. It was designed to give the animal exercise. However, I have to go retrieve the bowl out of the corner where Jasper has pushed it and place it back in the middle of the room. Sometimes I wonder who is really getting the exercise.

Touch is also a form of earthly spiritual communication. Touching, petting, kissing, and hugging are forms of spiritual communication where vocalization is not needed. Hugging is a way of telling someone that you care for them or that you love them without speaking. Petting your beloved animal is telling him or her that you love them. When your pet licks you or cuddles with you, this is a form of communication without talking. This spiritual communication is beneficial. When two people hug it benefits both people. It's the same as when petting an animal, both the animal and the person benefit. It is a mutual connection of the soul and benefits both participants. Be it human to human, animal to animal, or animal to human. A hug or a kiss gives the message that you love the person you are hugging or kissing without speaking. It is a non-verbal form of spiritual communication and the message is, "I love you." This also releases bodily chemicals such as serotonin and dopamine for both parties involved. These are healthy chemicals and they are *invisible* but they are real and they are earthly messages of a spiritual nature.

Let's look at some more invisible messages and messengers. Bodily chemicals and hormones send invisible messages to all parts of the body. Humans and animals use pheromones and body chemicals to communicate different messages such as when they are ready to mate or establishing territories. These invisible messages send information to the brain also. These invisible messages send instructions to our bodies in order to operate and stay healthy, such as chemical reactions that tell white blood cells to attack a virus. This is true for all living creatures and these chemical messages are frequencies and they are invisible. For centuries man did not know that the body had internal chemical messages because they could not see these chemicals and hormones. Scientists have proven that our feelings and emotions release chemicals in our bodies which are frequencies and they deliver information to our bodies, and the same applies to animals. Have you ever heard someone say that a dog can smell fear on you? It's true. Our bodies emit a chemical or frequency when we are scared and dogs and many other animals are able to smell. Dogs can also read fear by our body language.

Sign language and sound are also forms of communication used by humans and animals. Sign language is performed using the hands and fingers to communicate. Gorillas have been trained to use sign language to communicate with humans. And whales and dolphins have been trained to communicate through sounds.

During my time in the Navy I was a Communications Specialist. We utilized many different forms of communication such as land line, satellite, computer, paper-tape, teletype, card punch, voice scramble, morse code, and also electronic communications. All of these forms of communication are frequencies. And now most of us use electronic communication (e-mail). All these methods of communication work on frequencies and they are *invisible*. We can't see these electronic frequencies but they are there, and this is how the spirit world operates. It is invisible to us until we know and recognize the signs. As you can see, there are a myriad of invisible forms of spiritual communication both here on earth and from the afterlife.

Other forms of communicating without vocalization are: ships use flags to send messages, warnings, and vital information. Lights are used to signal other ships and tugboats use horns to communicate with each other. Think of a simple lighthouse that sends a message of danger with only a revolving bright light.

There are many, many ways of communicating here on earth and from the afterlife.

Since we will be dealing with the supernatural let's find out what this word means. Merriam-Webster defines this word as, *"Of or relating to an order of existence beyond the visible observable universe. Of or relating to God or a god, demigod, spirit, or devil. Departing from what is usual or normal, especially so as to appear to transcend the laws of nature. Attributed to an invisible agent such as a ghost, spirit, or God."*

An order of existence beyond the visible universe, relating to God or a spirit, departing from the normal, transcending the *laws of nature,* and attributed to an *invisible* agent. Remember these definitions as you read this book.

It is important to remember that voice communication is only one of many various methods of communication and that all messages and communications work on some type of frequency, and this also applies to the spiritual realm. We will now look at frequencies because frequencies have everything to do with entering into the spirit realm, which has *its own frequency.* And we know that many frequencies are invisible to us or as stated in the definition above, beyond the visible.

Below is a verse that tells us that heaven, spirits, and God are invisible.

> *"Now unto the King eternal, immortal, invisible, the only wise God, be honour and glory for ever and ever. A'-men." (1Timothy 1:17)*

Let's define the word invisible: *"Incapable by nature of being seen, not perceptible by vision, not visible to the eye." (Merriam-Webster)* Frequencies are invisible to humans as are many other things in this universe, and yet they are as real as you and I.

A German named Heinrich Hertz discovered frequencies and he is considered to be the father of frequencies. Both Albert Einstein and Nicola Tesla agree with Hertz that everything in the universe is composed of energy, vibration, and frequencies. A frequency is made up of vibrations and energy, and *everything* has a frequency which is known as the Resonant Frequency.

Scientists have proven that cats, dogs, and many other animals can see and hear frequencies of light and sound that humans are not able to see or hear. Infrasound is an audible frequency that humans can't hear, nor can humans see infrared light. We must utilize electronic equipment to detect some of these invisible frequencies. The spirit realm also has frequencies that we are unable to see or hear, but we can mentally and spiritually tune into these frequencies through prayer, dreams, and visions. And our animals can use these frequencies to send us signs and to communicate to us.

The frequencies we use to watch television and listen to the radio are invisible but they are *real*. We can't see them, but they are there. We can also use these invisible frequencies to communicate with our deceased animals. And our animals can also communicate with us using these frequencies through diverse types of signs and spiritual communications, which are all frequencies that we normally can't see or hear. Many people and some scientists believe that animals can see into the spirit world because they are attuned to the frequency of that world. Have you ever seen your dog stare at nothing and bark with their ears up? Or your cat meowing while looking into empty space? Of course you have.

Everything has a frequency and frequencies are used for *any and all* communications. Even light has a frequency. It wasn't too many years ago that we knew nothing of radio waves (frequencies). They are invisible and you cannot touch them, but yet they exist and we are using them today. We use them to bring signals to our televisions, radios, phones, and computers. Who would have thought this was possible not too long ago? The spirit world is invisible and we cannot touch it, yet it is real and it has its own frequency. It is on a different frequency that we can't see or hear unless we tune into that frequency, just as we can't see infrared light without special equipment. Our prayers and love are our special equipment. Frequencies can also be amplified and changed and some frequencies are addictive such as music and the love for our animals.

Spirits work on a different frequency that we cannot see or hear normally, but we can tune into these frequencies through prayer, visions, and dreams. It is truly a mysterious world and many people will try to say that they know everything when in reality, it is only their guess or opinion. And many choose to ignore these spiritual events, or call it imagination or crazy. Many years ago I did not believe in spiritual communication until it happened to me and it has happened more than once.

Have you ever walked into a room and you could feel the negativity in the air? You are feeling the spirit of anger, or the frequency of anger. We can also *feel* frequencies. You can't see this negative frequency, but you can feel it. Love is also a frequency and we can feel the love between ourselves and our animals, and also for humans that we care for. Think of how the frequency of a song you love affects your soul. You feel this frequency, or sound in your very spirit.

Your brain has five standard waves or frequencies which constantly change. Below are the frequencies that we use mostly on a daily/nightly basis but there are many more that will allow us to visit the afterlife:

1. Delta Wave – 0 Hz – 4 Hz
2. Theta Wave – 4 Hz – 8 Hz
3. Alfa Wave – 8 Hz – 12 Hz
4. Beta Wave – 12 Hz – 40 Hz (REM)
5. Gama Wave – 40 Hz – 100 Hz

These waves change throughout the day depending on our activity, moods, emotions, and feelings. Every soul/spirit has a frequency too. The human consciousness generates at a frequency of 0.5 Hz.

Spiritual growth is around 440 Hz which is also the Solfeggio frequency which is a meditation, relaxation, and also a healing frequency. This frequency is called the *Key of David*. King David played all the psalms in this heavenly frequency. When King Saul was possessed by a certain demon, David would play his harp in the solfeggio frequency and this frequency would drive the demon from Saul. David knew this frequency because he was close to God. God's frequency is 963 Hz. (FreqE1) Saul had disobeyed God and God had sent an evil spirit to vex him. In other words, Saul was possessed. In the next verse David plays the harp on God's frequency and drives the evil spirit from Saul.

> *"And it came to pass, when the evil spirit from God was upon Saul, that Da'-vid took an harp, and played with his hand: so Saul was refreshed, and was well, and the evil spirit departed from him." (1 Samuel 16:23)*

This verse tells us that the frequency of the Lord drove the demon out of Saul. It's all about the frequencies. There are frequencies that can drive evil away, but can also bring in our beloved pets from the afterlife through signs, dreams, visions, and spiritual manifestations.

Feelings, emotions, thoughts, and even love has a frequency. The frequency of love is 528 Hz. This frequency is also known as the miracle frequency and is used by many biochemists to repair DNA. (The OM Shopee.com)

There is an experiment called the *Chladni Experiment* which uses sand and frequencies to form complex geometric designs. This is called *Cymatics*. A tone generator is connected to a metal plate and sand is poured onto the plate. Certain frequencies vibrate the plate so that it creates areas that vibrate on the plate and also areas where there isn't any vibration. The sand falls into these non-vibrating areas forming beautiful geometric patterns. As the frequencies are raised it causes the areas of non-vibration to change, forming different and beautiful geometric patterns. (indierockcafe.com) The higher the frequency the more complex the mathematical geometric patterns become. Scientists and physicists have also proven that sound frequencies can move, levitate, and destroy objects. This is called *Acoustophoresis*. Frequencies are truly mysterious and scientists are only beginning to discover what they are capable of doing. But we know that these frequencies can allow us to contact and bring the spirits of our beloved pets from the afterlife.

Frequencies can be amplified. When two identical frequencies are coupled together they are amplified. Example: if two guitars are tuned and played at the same frequency the sound is amplified. The frequencies of your love and the love of your pet when put together are amplified and can bring the spirit of your beloved pet in from the afterlife. As King David drove the evil spirit away, God's frequency can also bring the spirit of your pet to you.

As you can see, our brain waves change with what we are doing and what feeling or mood we are in and also when we are sleeping and dreaming. Negative thoughts have been scientifically proven to lower your frequency which can cause one to become ill.

Not only are we able to change our frequency to different wavelengths, but we can also amplify our frequency. Frequencies are electro-magnetic waves and your brain omits 10-23 watts of power which is enough electric to power up a light bulb. Your love of Jesus and his love for you creates a spiritual power or frequency, and these two loves amplify the frequency. Then add the love between you and your beloved pet to that and it becomes even stronger and much more amplified. Through strong prayer I reached God's frequency and my spirit was taken to heaven and I saw Jesus, and he brought my dogs to me.

In this next verse Jesus himself tells us that he will come to us in a spiritual manifestation.

> *"He that hath my commandments, and*
> *keepeth them, he it is that loveth me:*
> *and he that loveth me shall be loved of*
> *my Father, and I will love him, and will*
> *manifest myself to him." (John 14:21)*

Let's define the word manifest so we will be sure to understand what Jesus is saying in the verse above. Webster's defines the word manifest as, *"Readily perceived by the eye. Clear or obvious to the eye and mind. To make evident. To show. Clearly apparent to the sight. To appear in visible form. To display or show by one's appearance." (p. 807)* Jesus is telling us that if we love him he will come to us in spirit form or in a spiritual manifestation. And this will also bring our beloved pet to us from the spirit realm if we ask.

Faith is a frequency and it generates at 528 Hz. God tells us that we must have faith if we want to have spiritual communication with him and our animals. The bible tells us this in the following verse.

> *"But without faith it is impossible to please him; for he that cometh to God must believe that he is, and that he is a rewarder of them that diligently seek him." (Hebrews 11:6)*

This verse tells us that we must be on the frequency of faith and that we will be rewarded in doing so. Love and faith coupled together can amplify your frequency. This means that we must believe in God with all our heart in order to reach the frequency of faith which will take us to heaven to see our pets. The above verse states that we must seek God diligently. The definition of the word diligent means, *"characterized by steady, earnest, and energetic effort." (Merriam-Webster)*

With every vision I have had, I had to relax and empty my mind and think only of Jesus. This changed my brain waves, or the frequency of my brain which connected me with God's frequency and into the frequency of the spirit world.

Now let's look at the different invisible frequencies that animals are able to see and hear, that we humans cannot see or hear.

Sight Frequencies:

Many animals are able to see ultraviolet light which is at the frequency range of 800 Terahertz to 30,000 Terahertz. They can also see infrared light which vibrates at 300 GHz to 400 Thz. The human eye can only see up to 60 Hz. We cannot see infrared or ultraviolet light, and yet many animals can.

Hearing Frequencies:

Dogs can hear up to 67 Hz – 45,000 Hz
Cats can hear up to 48 Hz – 85,000 Hz.
Bats can hear up to 110,000 Hz. (Petful.com)
The human ear can hear only up to 20,000 Hz.

Smelling frequencies: Smells are frequencies too.

A dog's sense of smell is 100,000 times stronger than that of a human.

A cat's sense of smell is about 14 times stronger than that of a human.

Cats, dogs, and many other animals can see ultraviolet light which is also known as black light. It is invisible to us because our eyes block out the ultraviolet light. There was a time when we did not know about these frequencies and many people did not even believe that these invisible frequencies existed. At one time it was science fiction and now science has proven it to be a fact. Think about this: Many animals knew that these frequencies existed long before man did because they use these frequencies every day.

Animals can see things that we can't and they can also hear things that we can't, because they are attuned to higher and lower frequencies than we are. We now know that these frequencies are there but we can't see them without special equipment, and yet animals can. Many animals can see infrared light which is electromagnetic radiation (EMR). It is invisible to us and yet it exists, and it is real. The EMR wavelength is much longer than visible light which is out of our frequency range. There truly is an invisible world that we are only now slowly discovering.

And now we have 5G which operates at a different frequency than all the previous modes. Most frequencies can pass *through* buildings and other obstacles. In reality, scientists really don't know much about frequencies. They only began to learn about them shortly before the advent of television and radio. So are we to believe that just because someone says we can't receive messages from the afterlife, this makes it true? I don't think so. The bible tells us that we can and now science tells us this too.

Think about this... if I had told you a hundred years ago that there would be a machine that would enable me to talk to you from a long distance using frequencies that you can't see, and that these frequencies could go through solid objects you would have called me a quack and locked me up in a mental institute for life. Now it has become reality. My point being, there are many things out there that we don't know about or fully understand. And there are also things in our mysterious universe that we can't see or hear...yet. This is how the spirit world is. Just because people can't see it does not mean it is not there. I have seen it and I know it is there. It's only a matter of reaching that frequency in order to see into the spirit world and to connect with God and your beloved pet. Learned men claim to know so much, but in reality the scientific knowledge of today is but a mere microbe in the vast ocean of unknown knowledge in this strange universe. The funny thing is that many discoveries over the years that scientists claim to have made have been in the bible for centuries!

Let's look at a simple example of something we can't hear but we know it is there. Most people are familiar with a dog whistle which omits a high frequency sound that dogs can hear, but we can't. Let's say that my grandson and I are out on the deck and I have a dog whistle. I blow on it and there is no noise. He won't believe that it's a whistle because he can't hear anything when I blow the whistle. Then I tell him that a dog can hear it and will respond if I blow the whistle because a dog can hear it, but we can't. He still wouldn't believe me. But if I brought Jasper outside with us and blew the whistle Japer would stand up stiff, his ears would come up, he would tilt his head and he would stare at me. Then my grandson would believe it because he *saw* the results. At first, he didn't believe that the whistle made any sound at all because he couldn't hear it, but it did make a sound whether he *heard it or not.* And once he saw the results of blowing the whistle he would then believe. And if my grandson told one of his friends about the whistle his friend would not believe him unless he too observed the results of the whistle being blown in front of a dog. This is how it is with us when we have a spiritual sign. No one believes us until they actually experience it for themselves. And if they have never experienced it they will laugh and call us crazy.

Here is another example: For hundreds of years sailors claimed that there was a giant, monstrous squid in the ocean. They called it a sea monster and everybody thought they were crazy and laughed at them, saying it was due to the fact that the sailors' imagination was affected by being at sea too long. A giant squid was found recently and now it has become truth. The squid measured 46 feet in length, and weighed almost one-thousand pounds with tenacles measuring 26 feet. The sailors were once crazy but now they aren't! Sometimes fiction *becomes reality.* My point is, just because some people don't see or hear something does not mean it isn't there, or that it isn't real.

God is a spirit and he has his own special frequency and dimension that allows him to pass through obstacles and dimensions. And we know frequencies and spirits can pass through solid objects. The bible has already informed us of this fact. Soon after Jesus rose from the dead he walked *through* the wall and into the room where the apostles were. This proves that God is a spirit and that he has a powerful frequency because frequencies can go through walls. And let's not forget he also walked on the water. The verse below tells us that he walked through the wall and the disciples witnessed this event.

> "Then the same day at evening, being
> the first day of the week, when the doors
> were shut where the disciples were
> assembled for fear of the Jews, came Je'-
> sus and stood in the midst, and saith unto
> them. Peace be with you." (John 20:19)

Jesus could do this because he is pure spirit and he has his own powerful frequency. He can enter into any dimension and pass through obstacles. Our deceased pets are now pure spirit and they have the ability to come into our dimension if God wishes it, or if we pray and we ask him to allow it. If you see your pet go through a wall or appear and disappear, you know that it is real because there is too much overwhelming proof that spirits can do this. You are not crazy.

Frequencies can also *transfer.* This is how GPS satellites work and also radar and sonar. These frequencies boom-a-rang through transference. These frequencies hit an object and they bounce back. They send and receive. The most simple example for frequency transfer is our phones. We transmit and receive frequencies (voice), on the phones that we use every day. How about email? We can send documents and pictures which are also frequency waves over the air from one place to another in a matter of seconds.

And Wi-Fi brings a signal (frequency) into your house via wire which goes into the router, which then shoots the signal out into the air throughout the house. This too is a form of frequency transference from wire and into the air. Did you know that rain can affect your internet reception? Rain is the same frequency as the internet frequency and the rain absorbs some of your signal (frequency.) This is called "rain fade." Frequencies are a true enigma that we are only beginning to understand. It's all about the frequencies!

So now we know that the frequency of your pet and your frequency can receive and transmit messages through these frequencies, be it audible or visual. Or in other words, we can hear and see the spirit of our beloved pets if we reach the correct frequency and have faith.

"For by him were all things created,
that are in heaven,
and that are on the earth, visible and invisible..."
(Colossians 1:16)

CHAPTER TWO

QUANTUM PHYSICS PROVES THE SPIRITS OF OUR PETS CAN SPIRITUALLY MANIFEST THEMSELVES

"If you talk to the Animals they will talk with you and you will know each other. If you do not talk to them, you will not know them, and what you do not know you will fear. What one fears, one destroys."
-Chief Dan George

Now let's look at some proven scientific facts concerning dimensions and the afterlife which are made up of frequencies that will prove that our animals can, and do send signs and manifest themselves to us. When I was in heaven God told me that BJ could be with me, my wife, and God at the same time in different places in heaven. He also told me that *everything* was connected to him.

As I researched and studied the CERN, quantum physics, and string theory I found out that it has finally been scientifically proven that there are other dimensions, and that everything is connected just as God told me over twelve years ago while I was in heaven. And it also proves that there is a heaven or another dimension, and that the spirits of our animals can come into our dimension and that we can also enter into their dimension through spiritual means. We will now look at quantum physics, string theory, and the CERN and see how they prove that there are dimensions other than the ones we are aware of. And that the spirits of our beloved pets can manifest themselves to us.

Quantum physics, string theory, and the CERN all state that there are other dimensions and that matter can exist in more than one dimension at the same time. This is called *Superposition* where matter does exist in *more than just one dimension.* In other words, matter can exist in more than one place or dimension at the same time, just as God told me. This also shows that NDE's, signs, dreams, visions, and spirit manifestations are very real occurrences.

Physicists have performed experiments where two atomic particles were separated from each other and a change in one particle created a simultaneous change in the other and it didn't matter if they were thousands, or millions of miles apart. This is called *Quantum*

Entanglement. This means that they are connected and they are one and the same, but in *different* locations. (NDE/Near-Death Experiences) This is what God told me years before science proved it.

These experiments have shown that there are other dimensions and both quantum physics and string theory state that there are at least ten dimensions. The bible and the book of Enoch tells us that there are ten layers, or dimensions in heaven. Science and the bible both tell us that it is completely possible for our beloved pets to come into our dimension and manifest themselves or send us signs. Science has now proven this with quantum physics. It also states that our "reality" is really only an illusion. String theory states that if a person or animal reaches a distance smaller than a millimeter, gravity will bleed them into another dimension. *This seems to fit the description of an animal or human spirit manifestation.*

The CERN has also proven there are other dimensions. You must remember that several of these dimensions contain demons. And they are able to come into our dimension if someone summons them through witchcraft such as a Ouija board, a ritual, a sacrifice, or any other demonic means which includes the CERN because they are bringing things into our world from other dimensions that don't belong here. So if one can summon demons through evil means, then it only goes to reason that we can summon angels and the spirits of our loved ones through prayers to God. In Ephesians the Apostle Paul tells us that evil spirits do roam the earth. He states that we wrestle not with flesh and blood, but with demons who rule the darkness of our world. Which he refers to as spiritual wickedness, or spiritual demon entities. In other words, he tells us without doubt that demon spirits are in this world. We see this in the next verse.

> "For we wrestle not against flesh and blood, but against principalities, against powers, against the rulers of the darkness of this world, against spiritual wickedness in high places." (Ephesians 6:12)

Paul even tells us to put on our spiritual armor against these evil spirits. He also states that these entities are spirits. And this spiritual armor is *invisible*, but Paul and many Christians believe that this armor exists and that it is real. I also believe this invisible armor is real.

Employees at the CERN have claimed that they have brought entities into our world and also sent things into another dimension. And it has been verified by some ex-employees that CERN is bringing evil spirits into our realm from another dimension. The director of CERN has openly and publicly stated that they are trying to bring something into our dimension from another dimension, and to send something into some other dimension. According to some ex-employees they have succeeded. Some think they are opening the bottomless pit mentioned in the book of Revelation. They are also trying to re-create the big bang to find the God particle. They are playing God and this can be very bad for us and the planet, not to mention the evil spirits they may be bringing into our dimension. Top physicists and scientists have warned them how destructive this could be but the people who work at the CERN do not care. I cover this in one of my books, *"How to Have Visions and Supernatural Knowledge in the Bible You Didn't Know Existed."* My point being, even the CERN has proven there are other dimensions and that it is possible to bring spirits from another dimension into our dimension and vice-versa, because *they have done it.* So now we know without a doubt that there are other dimensions and that spirits can come and go from one dimension to another. Science and the bible have both proven this.

Einstein's theory of relativity tells us that there is an invisible power that holds atoms together and that space and time are one unit and can bend and change.

We know that God is this invisible power that holds everything together. The verse below tells us this.

"And he is before all things, and
by him all things consist."
(Colossians 1:17)

If you see a spiritual manifestation of your beloved pet, or they appear and disappear through a wall or any other solid object, you will know it is not your imagination and that spirits can and will do this. They are on the frequency of the spirit world which is God's frequency and they are able to "bleed" into our dimension.

Both the bible and science have proven that NDE's, signs, dreams, visions, and spiritual manifestations are real events. And of course, God told us this in the bible thousands of years ago before man knew it.

In summary, Quantum physics states that the brain and physical body are composed of matter, atoms, and empty space. This is why our bodies can't go through solid objects. Only spirits can because they are pure spirit. The structure of atoms in our physical bodies are held together by atomic energy, but the soul and spirit are not physical they are pure spirit. Both science and the bible state that the spirit is separate from the physical body and that spirits are eternal. The spirit is *not* made up of matter, atoms, and empty space and is able to go through one dimension to another and also pass through obstacles. A spirit is made by the breath of God which is a piece of his spirit, and spirits are invisible. In other words, the soul or spirit is a separate entity from both the body and the brain. This is true for all living creatures.

...Is it mere coincidence that quantum physics, string theory, the CERN, the Book of Enoch, and the Bible all agree that there are ten dimensions?

"Your beloved animals
are not only waiting for you to join them,
they are expecting you."
-Steven H. Woodward

CHAPTER THREE

SIGNS, DREAMS, VISIONS, AND SPIRITUAL VISITATIONS

*"If all the beasts were gone, men would die
from a great loneliness of Spirit, for whatever
happens to the beasts also happens to man.
All things are connected. Whatever befalls
the earth befalls the sons of the earth."*
-Chief Seattle

According to Dr. James W. Goll there are twelve types of heavenly and prophetic *visions* that are in the bible. Dr. Goll states that visions are not just for prophets, but for ordinary people too. The twelve types of visions are listed below. Perhaps you have experienced one or more of these types of visions and were not aware of it.

1. *Spiritual Perception:* This type is a knowing or sensing of something good or bad. This is a

spiritual knowing. Some people call this intuition, discernment, or a gut feeling. An example would be if you feel the spirit of your pet and you know he or she is there with you. Or perhaps an inner voice that tells you something you didn't realize, and in your heart you know it is true.

2. *A Pictorial Vision:* This is when you see a picture in your mind of something, someone, or some place. This vision only lasts for a second or two.

3. *A Panoramic Vision:* This is when you see moving pictures in your mind of something, someone, or someplace. Or perhaps a prophetic vision.

4. *Dreams:* This occurs when one is sleeping and one has a dream of something divine, a prophecy, or perhaps a warning of some type. Dreams can also involve seeing and talking with your beloved pets or animals, people, or observing inanimate objects such as places, buildings, etc.

5. *An Audible Voice:* This type is when you hear an audible voice (or bark or meow, etc.) that may have saved your life or perhaps comforted you. God sometimes speaks in an audible voice. I have had this happen many times. An audible voice would also include hearing the spirit of your pet bark, meow, etc. Or your pet might make other sounds such as scratching, collar jingling, etc.

6. *Divine Sight:* Witnessing something that is supernatural such as a miracle. Or a prophetic seeing or sensing. Seeing Jesus or an angel. Also,

if you are looking at something or someone you can see their spirit. But most importantly, one example would be seeing your deceased pet which means you are seeing their spirit. Basically, divine sight is anything that is supernatural or of a spiritual nature and cannot be explained.

7. *A Heavenly Appearance:* This is when something, or someone, or your animal, or an angel, or even God himself appears to you. This can happen when you are asleep or awake.

8. *Open Heaven:* This type of vision is when God opens the heavens and you can see the heavenly realm or perhaps even see Jesus. Sometimes God will show a sign from heaven which could come in different forms such as the spirit of your beloved animal or any other spiritual vision. Saint Stephen saw heaven open up as he was being stoned to death. Or you may see signs in the clouds. I have seen some clouds that appear to be animals. I have seen pictures and videos of the sky where there appeared to be a figure walking that looked exactly like Jesus.

9. *A Trance:* A trance is a state of being just before a vision is given when one is in total worship to God. This makes one susceptible to open-eye (trance) visions like I have had. This happens when you are filled with the holy spirit.

10. *Translation:* This is when someone, or something is transported from one place to another and one doesn't know how or what happened to cause

this. Example: You can't find your car keys and then they appear on the kitchen counter even though you looked there twenty times already. Or perhaps one of your deceased pet's toys moved from the toy box to another place and you don't know how this happened.

11. *An Out-of-Body Experience:* This is basically an NDE (Near Death Experience). This happens when one dies for a short period of time and their spirit/soul leaves their body. It can also happen when one is in deep prayer and is given an open-eye vision. The spirit leaves the body and is taken to the heavenly realm and given divine information, or perhaps is met by a relative or pet. When I was taken to heaven in a vision my spirit was taken to heaven and my earthly body remained on earth, and I saw all my dogs in this heavenly realm.

12. *A Heavenly Visitation:* This is when one has a dream, vision, or NDE and you see your pet or a beloved family member. Or one could be taken to heaven and shown divine things such as the spirit of your deceased pet, angels, Jesus, or deceased relatives. This also includes a person being cured from some deadly disease during a visitation. And sometimes people are given important information or prophecies. It can happen when you are awake or asleep, during an NDE, and while dreaming or in a vision. I know that many of you have had this experience

and wondered if you were imagining it or just plain crazy. You are neither. This is a heavenly visitation! (Guideposts; Dr. James Goll.)

Don't be surprised if you see your beloved pet in a dream, a vision, or a spiritual manifestation. My wife has dreams and I have visions. Dreams can be vivid and they can seem very real and if you have had a vivid dream of your pet, than more than likely it was real and was sent to you from the afterlife by your pet! Or you may have had an open-trance vision of your pet. Or perhaps a sign that was to strange and obvious to brush off and you know in your soul that it was from your beloved animal from the spirit world, because it was too coincidental not to be real. Many people shrug these things off and miss the signs or they don't know what to look for. They don't believe that these spiritual things are possible and they think that these types of things are for crazy people. I remember as a young child that the idea of building a rocket ship and going to the moon was science fiction, or only something you read about in comic books or saw in the movies. Now it is reality.

Visions take much meditation and prayer but an open-eye vision is well worth the effort. Ask God for some kind of sign, dream, or vision and God will answer your prayers. He might not answer immediately, but he will answer in his time but you must look for and recognize the signs. And above all be patient. It took me three weeks of constant praying to receive my vision of BJ, and yet my first vision took only minutes. God tells us this in the following scripture.

"For the vision is yet for an appointed time, but at the end it shall speak, and not lie: though it tarry, wait for it: because it will surely come, it will not tarry."
(Habakkuk 2:3)

God is telling us that it will not tarry. The definition of tarry is, *"To wait." (Merriam-Webster)* And he also says it will surely come. It took me three weeks of constant praying and asking God for a sign to let me know if my dog BJ was in heaven or just a pile of dust and when I was about to give up, I was given a vision where I was taken to heaven and I saw and communicated with all my dogs.

There is a scripture that says to be still, listen, and seek God.

"Be still, and know that I am God…" (Psalm 46:10)

This means to empty your mind and concentrate on nothing but Jesus and what you desire. This will *change* and *amplify* your brain wave, or frequency. Ask him for what you want and he will give it to you, and sometimes he will give you much more than you could ever imagine. This includes signs, dreams, visions, and spiritual visitations from your beloved pet. But again, you must be patient and serious. And it will happen in a way that you never could imagine.

If you truly desire to communicate with your animal you must get close to God and connect with his frequency. Anything else is dangerous. Visions take lots of spiritual energy, but your unconditional love for your beloved pet has much energy and this love is enough to see into the spirit world. Love is a spirit and therefore it has energy and it is a frequency. Let's examine several examples of signs that your beloved pet is communicating with you. We will explore this in more detail in chapters four and eight.

A friend of mine lived in an old two-story house with wood floors. His faithful German Shepherd of fourteen years died of old age. His name was Harley and my friend said that he died in his arms. My friend lived alone. It was only himself and Harley, and he loved Harley like a son. About a month later I saw my friend and he said that sometimes at night he could hear Harley running around upstairs like he did when he was alive and when he would go upstairs to see what was going on, there was no one there. He knew it was Harley sending him a sign that he was still there. My friend has passed and I know that he is with his beloved Harley.

About six months after Petey passed we found one of Petey's favorite toys in the living room under the coffee table. We kept all his toys in a box in the back room. My wife and I asked each other if the other had put it there, but we had not. And we knew that BJ did not do it because the door to the room where Petey's toys were, was always kept shut. This was before my vision and at that time I really didn't give it much credence as I do today. After having my visions I know these things are real and I know now that it was a real sign from Petey.

Not long after BJ passed I awoke in the middle of the night and I heard his collar tags jingle and hitting up against his metal water bowl in the kitchen as though he were getting a drink of water like he did when he was alive. Three months after BJ passed I was on Facebook and I was contacted through the PM by a woman who had just lost her beloved dog. As we began to talk I got goosebumps. Her dog's name was BJ and he was a Shih-Tzu just like my BJ. I could ask for no better sign than that. As you can see, signs come in many, many different forms.

If a memory of your beloved pet comes to you out of the blue and you suddenly become emotional and perhaps start crying or become joyful, that is the spirit of your animal telling you that they are there with you. Their spirit is energy and you can *feel* it.

There are many people who have reported feeling their pet laying in the bed next to them. They have felt their pet brush up against some part of their body and snuggle up against them like they did when they were alive. Or they have felt their pet down by their feet and they see a depression on the bed where something was laying, or perhaps they feel a warm spot where one shouldn't be. These are spiritual visitations from your pet. Some people say that they get signs through a song on the radio, or something on television that will remind them of their pet.

I rarely listen to country music but I turned the radio on one day and it was tuned to a country station. I did not tune that channel in and I don't know how it got on a country station because I am the only one that drives that vehicle. When I turned the radio on I heard a song on the radio that I knew was BJ telling me not to be sad, reminding me that our relationship and the unconditional love that we shared was *well worth* the pain of loss.

If an animal comes to you in a strange manner shortly after the passing of your beloved, this is definitely a sign from your animal. I believe this is your beloved pet telling you to adopt and share your love with another animal.

You must be able to know and recognize these signs when they occur and know them for what they are. We have now seen the scientific proof concerning signs, spirits, and dimensions. Now we will examine the biblical scriptures that prove there is a spiritual realm and that our beloved animals can send us signs, visions, dreams, and spiritually manifest themselves to us.

"And a vision appeared to Paul in the night:
There stood a man of Mace-do'-ni-a,
and prayed him, saying,
come over into Mad-e-do'-ni-a and help us."
(Acts 16:9)

CHAPTER FOUR

BIBLICAL PROOF: GOD SENDS SIGNS, DREAMS, AND VISIONS FROM THE AFTERLIFE

*"Whom animals choose to
walk with are blessed."*
-Native American Proverb

Does this really happen? Does God really allow animals to bring us messages through signs, dreams, and does he allow our pets to visit us through visions in order to communicate with us? Does he send animal spiritual visitations to us? The answer is yes! The proof is in the bible. There were at least thirty people in the bible that had signs, visions, dreams, and spiritual visitations. And some of these people had more than one of these spiritual experiences. And many involved animals.

Throughout history God has sent messenger angels, spirits, and *animals* to deliver messages or to help people in their time of need through signs, dreams, visions, and spiritual visitations. He has sent earthly animals to help people and he has also sent messages to people using spiritual animals. God does these spiritual things in the bible so we know that it happens. God tells us plainly that he will do as he pleases which we see in the verse below.

> *"…My counsel shall stand, and I will*
> *do all my pleasure." (Isaiah 46:10)*

Now we will examine the biblical proof which coincides with much of the scientific facts we have read in chapter two. Throughout history God has sent both earthly and spiritual animals to help people and to deliver messages.

God Uses Earthly Animals. God has sent earthly animals to help people and also to deliver messages of great importance. The fish that God sent Jonah was special made or to be humorous, it was a special order fish. God made it right then and there.

God created and sent a big fish to save Jonah's life. Jonah would have died had it not been for one of God's animals. Due to this, Jonah was able to go to Nineveh where he saved thousands of people after being saved by a fish. The vast majority of people think it was a whale but it was not. It was a special fish God made to help Jonah. This fish came straight from heaven. Would this make the fish a spiritual animal since God made it on the spot? You decide.

> *"Now the LORD had prepared a great*
> *fish to swallow up Jo'-nah. And Jo'-*
> *nah was in the belly of the fish three*
> *days and three nights." (Jonah 1:17)*

God did this not only to save all the people of Nineveh, but also to save all the animals too. God sent a spiritual animal from heaven to save Jonah.

God Uses His Earthly Animals. God used his birds to feed Elijah and keep him alive in the wilderness. Elijah was on the run from King Ahab who wanted to kill him. Elijah hid out in the mountains by a brook and God sent earthly birds to feed him and keep him alive. God told these birds what he wanted them to do through *spiritual* communication which we see in the next verse.

> *"And it shall be, that thou shalt drink*
> *of the brook; and I have commanded*
> *the ravens to feed thee there…and the*
> *ravens brought him bread and flesh in the*
> *morning, and flesh in the evening; and he*
> *drank of the brook." (1 Kings 17:4 & 6)*

Audible Spirit Warning From an Animal. In this scripture Balaam's donkey stopped on the trail because she saw the angel of the Lord holding a sword and blocking the road. Balaam struck her three times to make her start walking again because Balaam could not see the angel. After being struck the donkey spoke to him. The Lord allowed Balaam's donkey to talk in order to save Balaam's life. The donkey could see the angel but Balaam could not. In this verse God is telling us that earthly animals *can see* into the spirit world. The donkey could see the angel but Balaam could not, until God opened his eyes to the spirit world. God gave Balaam spiritual eyes so that he could see the angel standing in his way and Balaam then realized that the donkey had saved his life.

> *"And the LORD opened the mouth of the
> ass, and she said unto Ba'-laam, what
> have I done to thee, that thou hast smitten
> me these three times? Then the LORD
> opened the eyes of Ba'-laam, and he saw
> the angel of the Lord standing in the way,
> and his sword drawn in his hand..."*
> *(Numbers 22:28-31)*

Then God told Balaam that he would have killed him, but would have saved the donkey!

Another important message in this verse is that God opened Balaam's eyes to the spirit world as God does for anyone who asks and he is also telling us that the donkey could see the angel but Balaam could not. This tells us that animals can see into the spirit world. Does this make animals more spiritual than us? I think so.

God Opens a Man's Eyes to the Spirit World. The king of Syria wanted Elisha killed because God was giving

Elisha directions where to find the Syrian army. This divine communication from God that was given to the prophet Elisha caused the Syrian army to continually lose battles against Israel. With this information Israel was able to surprise the Syrian army and defeat them. The Syrian king and his army finally found Elisha and they surrounded the place where Elisha and his servant were staying. In the morning when the servant woke up he went outside and he saw the king's army surrounding him and Elisha. Fearful, he ran back inside and told Elisha that they were surrounded and would surely be killed. Elisha told him not to fear because God's army was there and it was much larger and more powerful than the king's army. The servant could not see God's invisible army but Elisha could, for he was constantly on God's frequency. Elisha asked God to open up the eyes of his servant so that he could also see God's heavenly army that was surrounding the Syrian army. God opened up the eyes of the servant and he saw God's army. (Elisha was Elijah's protégé.)

"And when the servant of the man of God was risen early, and gone forth, behold, an host compassed the city both with horses and chariots. And his servant said unto him. Alas, my master! how shall we do? And he answered, Fear not: for they that be with us are more than they that be with them. And E-li'-sha prayed, and said, LORD, I pray thee, open his eyes, that he may

> *see. And the LORD opened the eyes of the*
> *young man; and he saw: and, behold, the*
> *mountain was full of horses and chariots of*
> *fire round about E-li'-sha." (2 Kings 6:15-17)*

In this last verse God opened the eyes of the servant so that he could see God's holy spirit army. The servant could see into the spirit world after God opened his eyes. This verse proves that God allows us to see into the spirit world if we desire it and ask. Elisha prayed for God to open up the spirit world to the young man and God did. I pray that God opens up the eyes to the spirit world of all who read this so that they too may see the spirit world and their beloved pets.

In this next verse God sends an angel with heavenly power food which consisted of bread from heaven and a jar of holy water.

> *"And as he lay and slept under a juniper*
> *tree, behold, then an angel touched him, and*
> *said unto him, Arise and eat. And he looked,*
> *and, behold, there was a cake baken on the*
> *coals, and a cruse of water at his head. And*
> *he did eat and drink, and laid him down*
> *again. And the angel of the LORD came*
> *again the second time, and touched him, and*
> *said, Arise and eat; because the journey is*
> *too great for thee. And he arose, and did eat*
> *and drink, and went in the strength of that*
> *meat forty days and forty nights unto Ho'-*
> *reb the mount of God." (1 Kings 19:5-8)*

These verses say a lot! First, an angel came to him from the spirit realm. Secondly, the angel touched him twice, and thirdly the angel brought him power food from heaven that sustained him for forty days and forty nights. Wish I could go that long without eating. Imagine the money you would save on groceries. And the angel even baked the bread for him. And lastly, this power food from heaven allowed Elijah to outrun a chariot. Talk about a power lunch!

And later God sent a heavenly chariot drawn by spirit horses to take Elijah to heaven while he was still alive. In this next verse Elijah and Elisha were walking together along the Jordan river when God sent a heavenly chariot of fire drawn by spirit horses to take Elijah to heaven and Elisha was a witness to this event.

> "And it came to pass, as they still went on, and talked, that, behold, there appeared a chariot of fire, and horses of fire, and parted them both asunder; and E-li'-jah went up by a whirlwind into heaven." (2 Kings 2:11)

Elijah was translated to heaven. This means he was taken to heaven while still alive. Enoch and Elijah were the only two humans to be translated. They were constantly on God's frequency.

An Open-Eye Vision of Many Spirit Animals. In this next verse the Apostle Peter was given an open-eye vision of many diverse animals that came from heaven to deliver an important message, and then they returned to heaven. God used many various spirit animals (that were once on earth) to deliver this message. You cannot deny the proof in the verse below that God sends spiritual animals to inform and help us. Notice it says that these animals *were* earthly animals. These animals were once on earth and had passed on and had gone to heaven and were now spirits. God tells us plainly in this verse that there *are* animals in heaven.

> *"…And saw heaven opened, and a certain vessel descending unto him, as it had been a great sheet knit at the four corners, and let down to earth: Wherein were all manner of four-footed beasts of the earth, and wild beasts, and creeping things, and fowls of the air…This was done thrice: and the vessel was received up again into heaven." (Acts 10:10-12&14)*

Please note that the verses above state that the animals came from heaven and were taken back to heaven. The message that God gave to Peter was that now all men were saved. This message was the second greatest message in human history and God chose many animal spirits to deliver it. So we see that God does allow the spirits of animals to come to earth for God's purpose. And if we pray and ask to see our beloved pets, God will allow this.

Open-Eye Vision: The bible tells us that dreams are *visions* when we sleep, or night visions. And open-eye visions are what occurs while we are *awake*. Visions (like I have had) are commonly called open-eye/open-trance visions as told in the book of Acts and also in the book of Numbers.

A passage from the book of Acts. Peter has an open-trance vision.

> *"And he became very hungry, and*
> *would have eaten: but while they made*
> *ready, he fell into a trance. And he saw*
> *Heaven opened..." (Acts 10:10-11)*

Also from the book of Numbers. Balaam has an open-trance vision.

> *"He hath said, which heard the words*
> *of God, and knew the knowledge of the*
> *most High, which saw the vision of the*
> *Almighty, falling into a trance, but having*
> *his eyes open." (Numbers24:16)*

An Open-Eye Vision. In this next verse we see Saint Stephen having an open-eye vision while being stoned to death. The people who were stoning him did not want to hear the truth that he was telling them and they ganged up on him and began stoning him. As he was being stoned, Stephen told them he saw heaven open up and he saw the glory of God and Jesus standing on the right side of God. They did not believe that he was having an open-eye vision of heaven, nor did they believe that he saw Jesus and God in the heavenly realm. And this made them even madder and they stoned him until he was dead. Notice he was full of the Holy Ghost (the frequency of God).

> *"But he, being full of the Ho'-ly Ghost, looked up stedfastly into heaven, and saw the glory of God, and Je'-sus standing on the right hand of God. And said, Behold, I see the heavens opened, and the Son of man standing on the right hand of God. Then they cried out with a loud voice, and stopped their ears, and ran upon him with one accord." (Acts 7:55-57)*

Dreams Of Prophecy. Joseph had a dream where he was told that he would be a great ruler one day and that all people would bow down to him.

> *"And he told it to his father, and to his brethren: and his father rebuked him, and said unto him. What is this dream that thou hast dreamed? Shall I and thy mother and thy brethren indeed come to bow down ourselves to thee to the earth?" (Genesis 37:10)*

And of course, his family did not believe him.

God Comes to Abraham in A Vision. In the next verse Abraham has a vision where God tells Abraham that he would bless him and make a great nation of him.

> *"After these things the word of the LORD came unto A'-bram in a vision, saying, Fear not, A'-bram: I am thy shield, and thy exceeding great reward." (Genesis 15:1)*

God Comes in a Night Vision to a Gentile With a Warning. When Abraham entered the land of Gerar he lied to King Abimelech and told him that Sarah was his sister because he was afraid that if the king knew that Sarah was his wife, the king would kill him and take Sarah. The king took Sarah thinking she was Abraham's sister and God came to the king in a dream that night to warn him that the king had taken Abraham's wife.

> *"But God came to A-bim'-e-lech in a dream by night, and said to him, Behold, thou art but a dead man, for the woman which thou hast taken; for she is a man's wife." (Genesis 20:3)*

King Abimelech gave Sarah back to Abraham and God did not kill him. But as we can see, God came to the king in a night vision to warn him and Abimelech was a gentile.

Dreams of Animals. God uses animals in dreams to deliver messages and warnings. God gave the pharaoh a prophetic dream using animals and Joseph interpreted the dream which not only saved the Egyptians from starvation, but also saved the Jewish nation.

> *"And it came to pass at the end of two full years, that Pha'-raoh dreamed: and, behold, he stood by the river. And behold, there came up out of the river seven, well favoured kine, and fatfleshed: and they fed in a meadow. And behold, seven other kine came up*

> *after them out of the river, ill favoured and*
> *leanfleshed: and stood by the other kine upon*
> *the brink of the river." (Genesis 41:1-3)*
> (Kine means cattle or cows.)

Pharaoh's dream involved cows. God used cows to warn the Egyptians that a seven-year drought was coming which saved their lives and continued the existence of the Jewish nation.

A Spiritual Visitation From Jesus in the Form of a Dream. This next verse shows that God not only gives dreams and visions but will answer our wishes and desires, and that sometimes Jesus will manifest himself to people.

> *"In Gib'-e-on the LORD appeared to Sol'-*
> *o-mon in a dream by night: and God said.*
> *Ask what I shall give thee." (1 Kings 3:5)*

God was telling Solomon that whatever he wanted he only had to ask for it and God would give it to him. God who is a spirit, came to Solomon in a dream. King Solomon knew the dream was real and told God he wanted wisdom which God gave him.

Dreams/Visions of Prophecy Using Animals. Daniel had many dreams and visions. And like Joseph, he interpreted the dreams of others that gave messages, warnings, prophecy, and help. Notice that Daniel says my vision by night which is a dream. In this next verse Daniel has a prophetic dream of the future concerning the End of the Age.

"Dan'-iel spake and said, I saw in my vision
by night, and, behold, the four winds of the
heaven strove upon the great sea. And four
great beasts came up from the sea, diverse
one from another. The first was like a lion,
and had eagle's wings: I beheld till the wings
thereof were plucked, and it was lifted up from
the earth, and made to stand upon the feet as
a man, and a man's heart was given to it."
(Daniel: 7:2-4)

There is more to this verse but I will not cite the entire narrative because it is too long. But you can get the gist of it. Daniel had several dreams and he also interpreted other people's dreams through God's spirit, or God's frequency. God used heavenly animals to send this message.

God Does Send Dreams and Visions. The next verse tells us that God sends dreams and visions to humans but many do not understand or believe. In the book of Job we see that God tells us that he does send dreams and visions.

"For God speaketh once, yea twice, yet
man perceiveth it not. In a dream, in a
vision of the night, when deep sleep falleth
upon men, in slumberings upon the bed:
Then he openeth the ears of men, and
sealeth their instructions." (Job 33:14-16)

The verse above says that if you believe and ask, God will give you signs, dreams, and visions. It also says that many who receive these signs ignore them or think it is only their imagination, or they just don't think these things are possible. People may say that these things only happen in the bible, or that they don't happen anymore. Doesn't the bible tell us that God *never* changes? Yes, it does. God tells us, "I am, that I am." This means that he does not evolve or change like we do. He doesn't have to evolve. He is the same always and he never changes. He is the beginning and the end. And God still sends dreams and visions to this very day.

Open-Eye Vision. Paul has an open-eye vision and is taken to heaven in this next verse.

> *"I knew a man in Christ above fourteen years ago, (whether in the body, I cannot tell; or whether out of the body, I cannot tell: God knoweth:) such an one caught up to the third heaven." (2 Corinthians 12:2)*

Many scholars believe that Paul was talking about himself but was too humble to say that it was he himself who was taken to heaven. Paul is telling us that he believed that when he was taken to heaven he was in his spirit body. Take notice that the verse says "third heaven" which is the third of ten dimensions/levels of heaven.

The ten levels of heaven according to Enoch are:

First Heaven: 200 angels govern over the stars.
Second Heaven: Where the dark angels are held.
Third Heaven: Where the Garden of Eden is located.

Fourth Heaven: It has its own sun that passes through 12 gates and is accompanied by angels.

Fifth Heaven: Where the fallen angels are kept.

Sixth Heaven: Where the Archangels reside and keep records of all human souls.

Seventh Heaven: Where all the other angels reside.

Eighth Heaven: This level is called Muzaloth. This is where the change of seasons, weather, and the twelve constellations are monitored.

Ninth Heaven: This is the home of the 12 constellations.

Tenth Heaven: This is where God resides with angels and *animals* (beasts) that sing and praise him eternally. *(Book of Enoch)*

Paul says he was taken to the third heaven. This is where I believe I was taken too. When I was in heaven I could not see or feel my body. I could only look forward and to each side. I had a panoramic view and I'm sure that my body was still in my chair while my spirit was in heaven. I also noticed that when I have my visions no one bothers me. It is as though God suspends time with my earthly body while my spirit is in heaven. In heaven there is no time or space as we know it. The beauty and peace is indescribable. Jesus told me that my pet could be with him, my wife, and me at the same time in different places when in heaven. In heaven, communication is by thought. It is not vocal and it is a far more intimate form of communication than talking.

When our beloved pets come to us whether it be

with signs, in dreams, visions, or manifested spiritual bodies they are in our dimension and also in the spiritual dimension. (Remember in chapter two where we saw that science calls this *Superposition* and *Quantum Entanglement*.) This is why they are fleeting images because it takes a lot of spiritual energy for them to come through. They are on God's frequency and this is why you may see them appear and disappear or go through a wall.

God definitely gives us signs. This is a fact because it tells us this all through the bible. Most all the old patriarchs had visions and dreams in both the Old and the New Testaments and it is still happening today.

Paul Brings a Man Back to Life: While Paul was preaching, a young man who was sitting in a window fell asleep and he fell out of the window to his death. Paul brought this man back to life. Please note that God gave all these saints the power to bring life/spirit back through their strong frequency of faith.

> *"And there sat in a window a certain young*
> *man named Eu'-ty-chus, being fallen into a*
> *deep sleep: and as Paul was long preaching,*
> *he sunk down with sleep, and fell down*
> *from the third loft, and was taken up dead.*
> *And Paul went down, and fell on him, and*
> *embracing him said, Trouble yourselves;*
> *for his life is in him." (Acts 20:9-10)*

Spiritual Signs in the Heavens. The next verse below shows us that God truly does send us signs, and this includes signs in the heavens too. He tells us so in the verses below. This is a prophetic verse.

"And there shall be signs in the sun, and in the moon, and in the stars; and upon the earth distress of nations, with perplexity; the sea and the waves roaring; Men's hearts failing them for fear, and looking after those things which are coming on the earth; for the powers of heaven shall be shaken." (Luke 21:25-26)

God uses a Star in the Heavens. God set the Star of Bethlehem in the sky for the three wise men to follow that took them to baby Jesus.

"Now when Je'-sus was born in Beth'-le-hem of Ju-dae'-a in the days of Her'-od the king, behold, there came wise men from the east to Je-ru'-sa-lem. Saying; Where is he that is born King of the Jews? For we have seen his star in the east, and are come to worship him." (Matthew 2:1-2)

God uses the Sun for a Sign. King Hezekiah had become deathly ill because he had disobeyed God. He then repented and asked for forgiveness which God granted him. He then asked the prophet Isaiah to ask the Lord if he would heal him from his sickness and Isaiah told the king that God said he would heal him. The king then asked for a sign from God to know for sure that God would indeed heal him. Isaiah told the king that God said he would make the shadow of the sun dial move as a sign. Isaiah then asked the king if he wanted God to move the shadow forwards or backwards. The king said that to move it forward would be too easy. The king told Isaiah to ask God to move it backward so he would know for sure. Isaiah then told the king that God would make the shadow go ten degrees backwards on the sundial as the king had asked.

> "And Hez-e-ki'-ah said unto I-sa'-iah, What shall be the sign that the LORD will heal me, and I shall go into the house of the LORD the third day. And I-sa'-iah said, This sign shalt thou have of the LORD, that the LORD will do the thing that he hath spoken; shall the shadow go forward ten degrees, or go back ten degrees? And Hez-e-ki'-ah answered, it is a light thing for the shadow to go down ten degrees; nay, but let the shadow return backward ten degrees. And I-sa'-iah the prophet crieth unto the LORD: and he brought the shadow ten degrees backward, by which it had gone down in the dial of A'-haz." (2 Kings 20:8-11)

In the last several verses God is telling us that he will, and does send signs to us from the heavens and the spiritual domain if we only ask. As you can see, God also uses the sun, the moon, and the stars to send us signs.

God Stops the Sun and the Moon. Joshua asked God to make the sun stand still so they could finish fighting their enemies the Amorites while there was light, because he knew they would lose the fight if it continued into the dark of night. The Amorites were a tribe of Nephilim. In Deuteronomy it states that these people were the last remnants of the giants. Their leader was a giant named Og and he was the Amorite king of Bashan. *(Deuteronomy 3:11)* His bed was 13-14 feet long and made of iron. I would have asked for more light too.

> *"Then spake Josh'-u-a to the LORD in the day when the LORD delivered up the Am'-o-rites before the children of Is'-ra-el, and he said in the sight of Is'-ra-el, Sun, stand thou still upon Gib'-e-on: and thou, Moon, in the valley of Aj'-a-lon. And the sun stood still, and the moon stayed, until the people had avenged themselves upon their enemies. Is not this written in the book of Ja'-sher? So the sun stood still in the midst of heaven, and hasted not to go down about a whole day." (Joshua 10:12-13)*

God made the moon and the sun stand still while Israel fought their foes and they won due to this miracle. Notice the verse says, "about a whole day." This will make sense in the next several paragraphs.

Joshua's long day has been confirmed by the historical records of almost every country in the world at that time in history. At that very date-year in time, Egypt, India, China, Persia, Peru, and the Aztecs, all recorded a long day. In North America the Indigenous people have an account of a long night and in South America, the Mexicans and the Mexican Indians tell of a long night also. And the list of countries documenting this phenomenon goes on and on. As you can see, Joshua's long day was recorded in almost every country around the world and at this time period, these people didn't know anything about Joshua. There is only one explanation; it really happened. The world verified it by the documentation in their own written histories.

And now NASA has also proven (by accident) that both Joshua's long day and King Hezekiah's sun dial account were real occurrences. NASA must calculate the days 1,000 years into the future before sending up a satellite because the orbits of the planets change and they wouldn't want to place a satellite in the future orbit of any of the planets because the satellites would be destroyed. While calculating time they were missing a whole day and they couldn't figure out why. They brought in a computer programmer and he said that the program was fine. They were baffled until someone mentioned the passage in the bible concerning Joshua's long day. They read the scripture and discovered that Joshua's long day was 23 hours and 20 minutes. But this still did not account for a full day. They were still missing forty minutes. Then someone mentioned King Hezekiah's account where the sundial moved backwards ten degrees. After reading King Hezekiah's occurrence they discovered that the sundial had moved backwards ten degrees which totaled forty minutes (ten degrees is forty minutes.) They added the hours and minutes together of both accounts and the calculations matched. So we have, 23 hours and 20 minutes, plus 40 minutes, which equals 24 hours. The two accounts added up to the missing full day! (Johnny A. Solbu) Do not be deceived my friends, the bible is as real as it gets.

A side note. Many of you who have read any of my books know that I speak of Canon-aid. Canon-aid books are considered biblically sound excellent reference material by most scholars. Canon-aid is any book written that is not in the bible but is spoken of in the bible, or was in our bible at one time. These books were removed over time for various reasons. Some were for nefarious reasons in order to discredit the bible and mislead people. The above scripture speaks of the book of Jasher. The book of Jasher, the book of Enoch, the book of Giants, the book of Maccabees, and several other books are all referred to in the bible and are considered Canon-aid. *Jesus also speaks* of these books and these people in the New Testament.

At one time these books were in the original bible but they were taken out. But they are still in the bible in several other countries, one being Ethiopia. Some of these books were also found among the dead sea scrolls. They are excellent reference materials for further study and research if you would like to read them. They have much spiritual information that you should know and will help you to understand the bible much better.

An Angel Manifests Himself to Joshua. In this next

verse an angel shows himself to Joshua. At first, Joshua didn't know who the angel was or if the angel was sent to help him, or fight against him. This particular angel was Jesus. Before Jesus came to earth he was the captain of all the angels. He was the captain of God's army. We know this was Jesus because he tells Joshua that he is standing on holy ground and Joshua worshiped him, and he tells Joshua that he is the captain of the Host of the Lord.

> *"And it came to pass, when Josh'-u-a was by Jer'-i-co, that he lifted up his eyes and looked and, behold, there stood a man over against him with his sword drawn in his hand; and Josh'-u-a went unto him, and said unto him, Art thou for us, or for our adversaries? And he said, Nay; but as captain of the host of the LORD am I now come. And Josh'-u-a fell on his face to the earth, and did worship, and said unto him, What saith my lord unto his servant? And the captain of the LORD's host said unto Josh'-u-a, Loose thy shoe from off thy foot; for the place whereon thou standest is holy. And Josh'-u-a did so." (Joshua 5:13-15)*

Jesus and Two Angels Visit Abraham. Let's don't forget the three angels that appeared to Abraham. And once again, one of these angels was Jesus because Abraham bowed to him and addressed him as Lord. Jesus and the two angels that accompanied him actually *sat, ate, and drank* with Abraham.

*"And the LORD appeared unto him in the
plains of Mam'-re: and he sat in the tent door
in the heat of the day; And he lift up his eyes
and looked, and, lo, three men stood by him;
and when he saw them, he ran to meet them
from the tent door, and bowed himself toward
the ground...and he stood by them under the
tree, and they did eat." (Genesis 18:1-2,8)*

A Spiritual Manifestation. In the book of Daniel
God sent a sign and a spiritual manifestation to King
Belshazzar. A hand appeared out of nowhere and wrote
a message on the wall directed to the king. This was
a spiritual manifestation or if you prefer, a spiritual
visitation.

*"In the same hour came forth fingers of a
man's hand, and wrote over against the
candlestick upon the plaister of the wall
of the king's palace: and the king saw the
part of the hand that wrote." (Daniel 5:5)*

After conquering Israel, King Belshazzar took many
of the holy objects from the Jewish temple for a party
he was throwing for all of his princes. He took the
holy golden vessels from the temple and he and his
guests were drinking wine from them. Those were
God's objects and it was God's hand that wrote on
the wall. The hand wrote, *"ME'-NE, ME'-NE, TE'-KEL,
U-PHAR'-SIN"* (Daniel 5:25) which means you and your
kingdom are finished, and you have been weighed in

the balance and have been found wanting. I will give your kingdom away. And that very night the king was killed and his kingdom fell to his enemy. That's where the saying, "the writing on the wall" comes from. Many of our sayings that we use today also come from the bible.

Belshazzar was the son of Nebuchadnezzar and God turned Nebuchadnezzar into an animal. Talk about supernatural!

> *"The same hour was the thing fulfilled upon*
> *Neb-u-chad-nez'-zr; and he was driven from*
> *men, and did eat grass as oxen, and his*
> *body was wet with the dew of heaven, till his*
> *hairs were grown like eagles' feathers, and*
> *his nails like birds' claws." (Daniel 4:33)*

The above verse also tells us that there is not much difference between animals and humans. And King Solomon tells us this too.

A Spiritual Sign. God gives Gideon a sign telling him that God will be with him in battle and that Gideon would be victorious.

> *"And Gid'-e-on said unto God, If thou wilt*
> *save Is'-ra-el by mine hand, as thou hast said.*
> *Behold, I will put a fleece of wool in the floor;*
> *and if the dew be on the fleece only, and it*
> *be dry upon all the earth beside, then shall*
> *I know that thou wilt save Is'-ra-el by mine*
> *hand, as thou hast said. And it was so: for he*

rose up early on the morrow, and thrust the
fleece together, and wringed the dew out of the
fleece, a bowl full of water." (Judges 6:36-38)

Gideon then asked God for a second sign which the Lord gave to him. And if you notice, it states that Gideon *asked* God for a sign.

Dreams and Visions. In the book of Numbers God tells us that he does give dreams and visions. This next verse is proof.

"And he said, Hear now my words: If there be
a prophet among you, I the LORD will make
myself known unto him in a vision, and will
speak unto him in a dream." (Numbers 12:6)

A prophet is anyone who believes in God, the Holy Spirit, and/or the spirit world. Animal lovers have a special spiritual insight because we *know* that animals have souls/spirits and we bond our spirits with the spirits of our animals.

Prophet: *"A person that is gifted with more than ordinary spiritual insight." (Merriam-Webster)*

We animal lovers know that our beloved pets have spirits and souls and that they can communicate to us from the afterlife through spiritual signs. Animal lovers are much more spiritual than non-animal lovers because we know they have spirits and we are able to bond our spirit with theirs. We have spiritual insight because we can see and feel the spirit of our animals. We are spiritual. We are spiritual prophets.

A Spiritual Visitation. The spirits of Moses and Elias appear to Jesus before the crucifixion.

> *"And after six days Je'-sus taketh Pe'-ter, and*
> *James, and John his brother, and bringeth*
> *them up into an high mountain apart, And*
> *was transfigured before them: and his face did*
> *shine as the sun, and his rainment was white*
> *as the light. And behold, there appeared unto*
> *them Mo'-ses and E-il'-as talking with him."*
> *(Matthew 17:1-3)*

Moses and Elias were *dead.* For a long time! The apostles were seeing two human spiritual manifestations. Many people say that people or animals don't, or cannot come back in spirit after they are dead. I guess they are wrong because the bible tells us differently. As you can clearly see, the spirits of Moses and Elias came back to earth in spiritual form in order to talk with Jesus before the crucifixion. And the apostles witnessed this.

Another Spiritual Manifestation. Here we have another verse that proves people do come back from the dead in spirit form if God allows it. The following verse is from the book of Samuel.

> *"And he said unto her, What form is he of?*
> *And she said, An old man cometh up; and he*
> *is covered with a mantle. And Saul perceived*
> *that it was Sam'-u-el, and he stooped with*
> *his face to the ground, and bowed himself.*

And Sam'-u-el said to Saul, Why hast thou
disquieted me, to bring me up? And Saul
answered, I am sore distressed; for the Phil'-
is-tines make war against me. And God is
departed from me, and answereth me no more,
neither by prophets, nor by dreams: therefore I
have called thee, that thou mayest make known
to me what I shall do." (1 Samuel 28:14-15)

Samuel was dead but God allowed Saul to summon Samuel's spirit (through the witch of Endor.) Saul states that he was not getting advice from prophets and dreams any longer because he had disobeyed and forsaken God.

Some people will say that in the above verse the spirit of Samuel was a demon acting like he was Samuel because it says that Samuel asked Saul, "why did you bring me up?" But if you have read the bible you will know that at that time paradise was down below next to hell, until Jesus went down and brought all the Old Testament saints that had died, *up* from paradise into heaven. So Samuel came *up* from paradise, not hell. And if you notice, it states that Samuel was covered with a mantel. Only people of God wear a mantel. The mantel is from God and many of God's prophets wore a mantel. A mantle is a holy robe or cloak that is given by God which some believe is a symbol of the holy spirit which gives supernatural powers from God. Elijah wore a mantel and performed miracles and when Elisha took Elijah's mantel, he began to do twice the miracles that Elijah performed because he asked God for a double portion of what Elijah had. Both of these mighty prophets brought people back from the grave. The verse above states that the spirit of Samuel was covered with a mantel. Demons don't have mantels. It also states that Saul "perceived" that is was Samuel. Merriam-Webster defines the word perceived as, *"To become aware of directly through any of the senses, especially sight and hearing."* Saul knew Samuel by sight and he recognized his voice.

Elijah Brings a Child Back to Life. Elijah and Elisha both brought people back from the dead. A poor widow woman helped Elijah by feeding him and she had also given him a place to stay because she knew he was a man of God. When her only son died she begged Elijah to bring him back to life. And he did.

> *"And it came to pass after these things,*
> *that the son of the woman, the mistress*
> *of the house, fell sick; and his sickness*
> *was so sore, that there was no breath left*
> *in him. And then she said unto E-li'-jah,*
> *What have I to do with thee, Oh thou man*
> *of God? art thou come unto me to call my*
> *sin to remembrance, and to slay my son?*
> *And he cried unto the LORD, and said, O*
> *LORD my God hast thou also brought evil*
> *upon the widow with whom I sojourn by*
> *slaying her son? And he stretched himself*
> *upon the child three times, and cried unto*

the LORD, and said, O LORD my God, I
pray thee let this child's soul come into him
again. And the LORD heard the voice of E-li'-
jah; and the soul of the child came into him
again, and he revived." (1 Kings: 17-22)

In this last verse Elijah actually brought the dead boy back to life the same as when Jesus brought Lazarus back from the dead. If you notice it says that the boy's soul returned to his body. And please note that Elijah stretched his body over the child three times. Three is God's number for holy.

Elisha Brings a Child Back to Life. Let's look at another event where the soul has left the body and then returned. Or in other words, someone was brought back from the dead and the soul returned to the body. In this scripture Elisha brings a child back to life.

"And when E-li'-sha was come into the house,
behold, the child was dead, and laid upon his
bed. He went in therefore, and shut the door
upon them twain, and prayed unto the LORD.
And he went up, and lay upon the child, and
put his mouth upon his mouth, and his eyes
upon his eyes, and his hands upon his hands;
and he stretched himself upon the child; and
the flesh of the child waxed warm. Then he
returned, and walked in the house to and
fro; and went up, and stretched himself upon
him: and the child sneezed seven times, and
the child opened his eyes." (2 Kings: 32-35)

Elijah and Elisha were true men of God and were constantly on God's frequency, and they both wore the mantle of God.

Peter Brings a Woman Back to Life: In the book of acts the Apostle Peter brings a godly woman named Tabitha back to life. She was a disciple and she did many good works for the Lord. Peter brought her soul back to her body.

> *"But Pe'-ter put them all forth, kneeled*
> *down, and prayed; and turning him*
> *the body said, Tab'-i-tha arise. And she*
> *opened her eyes: and when she saw*
> *Pe'-ter, she sat up. (Acts 9:40)*

Many People (Saints) Arise from the Grave: In the book of Matthew it states that many of the dead saints rose from the grave right after Jesus died on the cross. And many people were witness to this supernatural event.

> *"Je'-sus, when he had cried again with a loud*
> *voice, yielded up the ghost. And, behold, the*
> *veil of the temple was rent in twain from the*
> *top to the bottom; and the earth did quake, and*
> *the rocks rent; And the graves were opened;*
> *and many bodies of the saints which slept*
> *arose. And came out of the graves after his*
> *resurrection, and went into the holy city, and*
> *appeared unto many." (Matthew 27:50-53)*

A Special Proof of Transference: Here is the example I spoke of in chapter one where frequencies are able to transfer. This verse tells us that frequencies can transfer (send and receive) from the spirit world and we can send and receive messages to them into the spirit dimension. It also proves again that God does allow the spirit to leave heaven and come back to the living. In this next verse a man's spirit returns to his body and he lives once again. In the verse below, a man has died and they lower him into Elisha's grave. When the dead man's body touched the bones of Elisha he came back to life. God allowed the frequency to remain in Elisha's bones so that when the dead man's body touched Elisha's bones, his spirit returned to his body. God allowed the frequency of Elisha's spirit (which is really God's spirit) to transfer from his bones to the dead man's body, which brought the dead man back to life.

> *"And it came to pass, as they were burying a man, that, behold, they spied a band of men; and they cast the man into the sepulchre of E-li'-sha: and when the man was let down, and touched the bones of E-li'-sha, he revived, and stood up on his feet." (2 Kings13:21)*

Enoch Goes to Heaven and Back: In the book of Enoch it says that Enoch was taken to heaven and shown all the mysteries of heaven and then God returned him to earth to tell his family of his time in heaven and to write down all he saw and heard. Enoch then told his family good-bye and God took him again never to return. Some think Enoch and Elijah will be the two witnesses spoken of in Revelation. I believe this because God says that all men must suffer death and Enoch and Elijah were taken to heaven while still alive. They have never died. But the two witnesses will die after a period of time during the end of the age.

A Spirit Visits Job. In the next verse God sends a spirit to Job.

> *"Now a thing was secretly brought to me, and*
> *mine ear received a little thereof. In thoughts*
> *from the visions of the night, when deep*
> *sleep falleth on men. Fear came upon me,*
> *and trembling, which made all my bones to*
> *shake. Then a spirit passed before my face:*
> *the hair of my flesh stood up: It stood still,*
> *but I could not discern the form thereof: an*
> *image was before mine eyes, there was silence,*
> *and I heard a voice, saying..." (Job 4:12-16)*

Does this sound familiar? How many of you have had this same experience? Seeing a fleeting image of your beloved pet, or perhaps you have heard a distant bark, meow, or some other strange sound or incident you couldn't explain that you knew was your beloved pet? When God sends a spirit it can be either human or animal.

A Spiritual Night Vision/Dream. In this next verse God talks to Jacob in a night vision. Remember, a night vision is a dream. He tells Jacob to go to Egypt and that he will make Jacob's people into a great nation. And if you remember, God had changed Jacob's name to Israel.

*"And God spake unto Is'-ra-el in the visions
of the night, and said, Ja'-cob, Ja'-cob. And he
said, here I am. And he said, I am God, the God
of thy father: fear not to go down into E'-gypt;
for I will there make of thee a great nation."
(Genesis 46:2-3)*

In the last verse Jacob receives a promise from God in an audible voice and through a dream which we know is a heavenly visitation.

A Spiritual Sign and a Spiritual Visitation. In the book of Acts the disciples were recounting the events of Moses to the people. Moses had killed a man and then he ran away into the desert where he encountered a sign, an angel, and also God himself.

"Wilt thou kill me, as thou diddest the E-gyp'-tian yesterday? Then fled Mo'-ses at this saying, and was a stranger in the land of Ma'-di-an, where he begat two sons. And when forty years were expired, there appeared to him in the wilderness of mount Si'-na an angel of the Lord in a flame of fire in a bush. When Mo'-ses saw it, he wondered at the sight: and as he drew near to behold it, the voice of the Lord came unto him." (Acts7:28-31)

The Lord sent Moses an angel messenger, a sign in the form of a burning bush, and God also talked to him in an audible voice.

Angels/Spirits Walk the Earth. In the book of Hebrews the Apostle Paul tells us that angels are here on the earth. And we know that angels are spirits. It also tells us that spirits can take human form and we know that God sends spirits in the form of animals too, as we have seen in the verses that we have covered so far.

"Be not forgetful to entertain strangers:
for thereby some have entertained
angels unawares." (Hebrews 13:2)

It is true, angels and spirits do walk the earth and they watch over us because the bible verse above tells us this. Angels are spirits and if God sends angels to earth, why would he not send animal spirits to help? He does! But beware. Angels walk the earth, but so do demons because the bible tells us this.

God Does Talk to Us. God *wrestled* and talked with Jacob. God talked to Moses on Mount Sinai and was given an epic mission into Egypt to free the Jewish nation. Abraham fed God and he also *negotiated* with God to save some of the people in Sodom and Gomorrah before God destroyed it. And God talked to Solomon and many of the other prophets. God has always talked to his prophets and those who believe in him. And he still does in some form or other.

So now we see that the spirits of people and animals can, and do come back from death through manifesting their spirit to us if God allows it because the bible tells us this. In the bible there are a total of *ten* people that were brought back from the dead.

As you can clearly see, spiritual signs are real and

God will give us these things if we only ask him through prayer. The verse below states this.

"But if from thence thou shalt seek the
LORD thy God, thou shall find him, if
thou seek him with all thy heart and with
all thy soul." (Deuteronomy 4:29)

Seek the Lord with all your heart and soul and he will send your beloved pet to you in a dream, vision, or a spiritual visitation.

God tells us that he does allow the spirit to return in the next verse.

"The LORD killeth, and maketh alive: he bringeth
down to the grave, and bringeth up." (1 Samuel 2:6)

In the verse above it says that God will bring down to the grave and bring up from the grave. Some will say that the above verse means that God will give eternal life in saying that he will bring up from the grave. However, many of the bible verses are *polysemous* which means that they have multiple meanings. This verse does mean that God gives eternal life by resurrection from the grave after death. But it also means that he allows the spirit of your deceased animal to visit you in spirit form, as we have proven in the preceding verses that we have read. In other words, the verse says that God will do *whatever pleases him*. God can do anything he desires. This includes allowing spiritual visitations from deceased animals or relatives if we go through God.

Jesus Appears After the Resurrection: Did you know that Jesus appeared to the disciples three times after he rose from the grave? To God, the number three means holy and sacred.

> *"This is now the third time that Je'-sus shewed himself to his disciples, after that he was risen from the dead." (John 21:14)*

God Spiritually Commands His Lions. In the verse below Daniel has been set up by corrupt prophets. They were jealous of him because King Darius liked him and because he was a Jew. Daniel has been thrown into a den of hungry lions. The king did not want to put him in the den, but was forced to because he was tricked into signing a decree that sealed Daniel's fate. The following morning the king ran down to see if Daniel was dead or alive. If he were alive then the king would know that Daniel's god was the one true god. These lions would have eaten anyone else.

> *"Then the king arose very early in the morning, and went in haste unto the den of lions. And when he came to the den, he cried with a lamentable voice unto Dan'-iel: and the king spake and said to Dan'-iel, O Dan'-iel, servant of the living God, is thy God, whom thou servest continually, able to deliver thee from the lions? Then said Dan'-iel unto the king, O king, live for ever. My God hath sent his angel, and hath shut the lions' mouths, that they have not hurt me: forasmuch*

as before him innocency was found in me; and also before thee, O king, have I done no hurt."
(Daniel 6:19-22)

Daniel said he had done no wrong to god, or to the king. I have a feeling that the angel mentioned in this verse is none other than Jesus. This leads us into another story that has happened recently.

Animals Appear Out of Nowhere to Save Humans. To show that these things still happen today, below is only one of thousands of stories where animals have saved humans throughout history. However, this is most recent. Again as with Daniel, God used lions to protect a pastor on Easter Sunday a few years ago. This happened in the Middle East and what is strange about this story is that these animals appeared out of thin air where they were not supposed to be. And then they vanished.

A pastor and several of his friends were in the Middle East preaching the Gospel and were attacked by a group of terrorists. Suddenly out of nowhere, several lions appeared from out of the tree line and attacked the terrorists. When the terrorists tried to kill the lions, more lions showed up and ran the terrorists away, saving the pastor and his friends. After running the terrorists away the lions left and disappeared back into the grove of trees. The lions didn't bother the pastor and his friends. (Christian Headlines)

What were these lions doing in that part of the Middle East? There were no lions ever known to have been in that part of the country. Where did they come from? Were these animal spirits sent by God in the form of lions to save a man of God like when God sent a fish to save Jonah? God still sends signs and miracles, and he still uses his animals.

A Warning From Jesus. Again, you must ask the Lord for any spiritual signs. Jesus gives us this warning in the book of John.

> *"Beloved, believe not every spirit, but*
> *try the spirits whether they are of God:*
> *because many false prophets are gone*
> *out into the world." (1 John 4:1)*

God is telling us that there are spirits both good and bad that roam the earth and that they can manifest themselves to us. God is also warning us to ask for signs from him and no one else. We must ask God for these things. God gives signs, dreams, visions, and spiritual visitations, but so does Satan. God is telling us that he *does* send spiritual signs to us if we ask him, and only him. And sometimes God sends these signs when we don't ask.

*"For with God
nothing shall be impossible."
(Luke 1:37)*

CHAPTER FIVE

BIBLICAL PROOF: GOD WANTS US TO ASK HIM FOR SIGNS FROM THE AFTERLIFE

*"All things share the same breath – the
beast, the tree, the man. The air shares
its spirit with all the life it supports."*
-Chief Seattle

God Sends dreams and visions if we ask. The scriptures tell us that God does communicate to us through dreams and visions, and that he also *wants* us to ask him for these things as shown in the following verses.

God Wants Us to Ask For Signs. In the book of Proverbs God tells us that he wants us to communicate with him into the afterlife.

"Yea, if thou criest after knowledge, and liftest up they voice for understanding...Then shalt thou understand the fear of the LORD, and find the knowledge of God." (Proverbs 2:3-5)

In this last verse God is telling us that if we pray, he will allow us to communicate with him and our beloved animals. The spiritual afterlife is the knowledge of God. He is the afterlife and the spiritual knowledge.

Proof There is Spiritual Communication. The next verse tells us plainly that we can communicate into the spirit world. It tells us that we must use spiritual communication into the afterlife to speak with God and our beloved pets. It also states that some people do not believe that there is a spiritual form of communication.

"...the words that I speak unto you, they are spirit, and they are life. But there are some of you that believe not." (John 6:63)

God Will Give Us What We Desire. The next verse below tells us that he will give us what we want if we only ask him.

"He shall pray unto God, and he will be favourable unto him: and he shall see his face with joy: for he will render unto man his righteousness." (Job 33:26)

The word render means to *"To pay back, to furnish, to deliver, to surrender." (Merriam-Webster)* The word favorable means, *"Expressing approval. Giving consent."*

(Merriam-Webster) This tells us that God approves of us asking him for spiritual signs and that he will give us (render) what we ask. And it also states that God not only approves of us asking, but he wants us to ask and that he will consent to our prayers and wishes. God is telling us that if we ask in serious prayer he will give us what we desire, and God also desires that we talk to him. Ask him for a sign, dream, vision, or spiritual visitation from your beloved pet. But you must know Jesus on a personal level. The next verse also tells us that God will give us what we desire.

> *"Delight thyself also in the LORD;*
> *and he shall give thee the desires*
> *of thine heart." (Psalm 37:4)*

This verse tells us without any doubt that God will give us what we desire. Don't we desire with all our heart to see our beloved pet again? Yes we do.

God Will Bring You to His Frequency. In the verse below God says he will fill you with his spirit and send you a spiritual sign or visitation from your beloved pet. He will share the secrets of heaven with you.

> *"Turn you at my reproof: behold, I will pour*
> *out my spirit unto you. I will make known*
> *my words unto you." (Proverbs 1:23)*

In this last verse God is telling us that he will fill us with his spirit or his frequency if we only ask. And he will open up the spirit world to us. Or in other words, we will be on his frequency and he will send spiritual signs, dreams, and visions. You will know when you are filled with the spirit because you will feel a peace and contentment that is beyond description. You will also feel a love that is so powerful you will cry like a baby.

God Tells Us to Ask For Signs. The next verse below is more proof that God wants us to ask for spiritual signs. But you must believe in God and believe that he does send these things to us. Spiritual signs are wisdom and they are revelation. The next verse states, "in the knowledge of him." This means that you must *personally know* him, and it also means that he will share his knowledge and revelations with you, which includes spiritual signs, visions, dreams, and spiritual manifestations of your beloved pet.

"That the God of our Lord Je´-sus
Christ, the father of glory, may give
unto you the spirit of wisdom and
revelation in the knowledge of him."
(Ephesians 1:17)

God is telling us to ask him for signs and if you notice, it says the spirit of wisdom. This verse plainly tells us that wisdom is a spirit and dreams, visions, signs, and spiritual visitations are all spiritual communications and wisdom. Let's examine the meaning of the word revelation that we see in the verse above. Webster's dictionary defines it as: *"An instance of something communicated or disclosed. Something revealed. Something not before realized." (p.1129)* Read the definition of the word revelation carefully. It says, "something communicated, something revealed, something not before realized." God is talking about spiritual communication with him and spiritual signs and manifestations.

The great thing about asking God for a sign, vision, or a dream is that you can ask for any specific thing you want. I asked to see my beloved BJ and I saw all of my dogs. I saw no humans because I didn't ask, nor did I care to see any humans. I only wanted to see BJ and God allowed me to see all my dogs. He always gives me much more than what I ask for. If you would like to read the whole story of my trip to heaven please read the book, *"Biblical Proof Animals Do Go To Heaven."* The real BJ is the little Shih-Tzu on the cover of the book.

Jesus Says We Can Have Dreams and Visions: In the next verse we can see that Jesus is telling us that we are capable of having dreams, visions, signs, and spiritual visitations.

> *"Verily, verily, I say unto you, He that believeth*
> *on me, the works that I do shall he do also;*
> *and greater works than these shall he do;*
> *because now I go unto my Father." (John14:12)*

Jesus did all these things and he tells us that we can do these things and *much more*. Notice that the verse says he is going to his father. This means that the father (God) is where all the power comes from for us to do these divine things.

God sends dreams and visions to humans but many people don't listen and they shirk it off because they think it is nonsense or they just don't believe in those things. And some don't believe in God either. In reality, God does speak to us through signs, dreams, and visions. And he does send animals to us in dreams, visions, and spiritual visitations from the spirit world or what I call heaven. And sometimes he takes our spirit to heaven. So now we see that God sends messages to us through human and animal spirit manifestations, signs, dreams, and visions. The greatest *sign* God sent us was the Star of Bethlehem. The next greatest sign was the Rainbow.

Most all of the patriarchs in the bible had dreams, visions, spiritual visitations, and signs from animals, angels, and God. Many of these dreams and visions had animals in them. Some of these patriarchs are, Abraham, Moses, Job, Jacob, Gideon, Samuel, Isaiah, Ezekiel, Daniel, Amos, Zechariah, Matthew, Paul, Peter, John the Revelator, and many of the gentiles that these patriarchs dealt with such as, pharaohs, and kings.

*"The last enemy
that shall be destroyed is death."
(1 Corinthians 15:3)*

CHAPTER SIX

MORE PROOF OF THE SPIRIT WORLD: NEAR DEATH EXPERIENCES

"Upon death, the soul flies free
...and enters into eternity."
-Steven H. Woodward

Millions of people have had NDE's (Near Death Experiences). There are over nine million people who have reported experiencing an NDE. And we don't know how many NDE experiences have occurred that have never been reported for fear of ridicule.

This phenomenon happens when a person dies for a short period of time and comes back to life either on their own, or resuscitated by a doctor. These people claim that they went to heaven in the short time that they were clinically dead. They claim to have seen loved ones who have passed and they also state that they have seen animals. And many have said that they saw their own animals in heaven. These events are life-changing experiences for those who have had these spiritual experiences. One lady said that her dog was the first to greet her when she arrived in heaven. Her dog was the *first* to greet her in heaven before anyone, or anything.

When people die the brain ceases all activity and during this short period of time that they are clinically dead, they say that they are completely free of pain and their minds are clear and operate much faster than normal. They have a sense of clarity, overwhelming peace, and they feel an intense unconditional love surrounding them. They claim to have unlimited knowledge and sometimes one sees the future or the past, and they also state that they have seen their deceased relatives and animals. When I was in heaven and saw BJ I could see the vast knowledge in his eyes. I felt inferior to him because I knew that his knowledge far surpassed my own. I knew that he knew all the secrets of the universe and that it all came from God.

Some state that they have the feeling of floating above their bodies from the area of the ceiling. They observe not only their bodies but also all the actions and conversations of those that are present in the room such as doctors, nurses, or family members. Some describe traveling through a tunnel that leads to a bright light and some say that they were taken straight to heaven and have interacted with their pets and relatives. Sometimes they are told that it isn't their time yet and that they must return, or they are given the choice to stay in heaven or return to their earthly bodies. And some state that they went to hell and were rescued by Jesus.

Many times, these people have given testimonies that cannot be disputed. A Veridical NDE is where a person is able to describe events and conversations that transpired while they were dead. For instance, they can describe the actions of people in the room, what was said, and also describe items that were in the room that they could not have possibly known about while they were clinically dead. In many cases people were able to describe the operating tools used and the conversations of the doctors in the operating room while they were dead.

Others have claimed that they traveled to a distant place and can describe this place in detail having never been there before. One boy who had an NDE claimed that he met a relative in heaven that he had never known about or had never seen or met. Nor had he ever been told about this relative and yet he described the relative in detail. When his parents showed him a picture of this relative in a photo book of many other people the boy picked out the correct picture. This is more than coincidence; it is indisputable proof. Many people who have had an NDE claimed they went to heaven and saw Jesus and upon their return they were healed from a terminal illness, which completely baffled the doctors. The doctors were unable to explain this except to say that it was a miracle.

Many skeptics who have had NDE's have converted to Christianity after having this experience. Of course there are some who make these stories up, but the majority are true due to the proof that is undeniable through veridical NDE's. I give much more detail of NDE's in my book, *"How to Recover From the Heartbreak of Pet Loss"* which includes stories of people who saw their animals in heaven during an NDE.

Scientists and psychiatrists *cannot* prove that these NDE experiences are not true divine events. Their theories are only opinions. They have no proof whatsoever, nor have they been able to explain how these people who have had vertical NDE's are able to describe items in the room, or the actions and the conversations of the people in the room that occurred while they were deceased. Or in cases where people who had maladies or terminal illnesses were completely cured after their experience. The fact is, those who claim that NDE's are not real have *no proof* whatsoever. Those who have had vertical NDE's can prove it is true by knowing and describing things that they could not possibly have known while dead. NDE's are a sign or a spiritual experience which must be included with visions, dreams, and spiritual visitations. All of these events are spiritual communications given by God.

So who shall we believe? Men who claim to be wise and educated that are full of arrogance and greed to receive funds for their agenda. Or perhaps arrogant false prophets who don't know the true word of God? Or atheists who don't know or believe in God, and they think because they have degrees that this makes them God? What does the bible say about these types of people?

> *"Professing themselves to be*
> *wise, they became fools."*
> *(Romans 1:22)*

Or do we believe the people who have had these experiences and have indisputable proof? I will believe the word of God which tells us that our pets have souls and are in heaven, and that God does communicate to us through spiritual means. Our beloved pets can send us signs from the afterlife because the bible tells us this and I have faith in God, not man.

> *"For therein is the righteousness of*
> *God revealed from faith to faith: as it is*
> *written. The just shall live by faith."*
> *(Romans 1:17)*

"I know that whatever God doeth,
it shall last for ever..."
(Ecclesiastes 3:14)

CHAPTER SEVEN

THE SOULS OF ANIMALS AND THE AFTERLIFE

"To bond our soul with an animal's
soul is a sacred and precious gift.
It is a special privilege given to us by God
...that many do not have."
-Steven H. Woodward

In several of my books I have proven that animals do have souls and that they do go to heaven through both scientific facts and biblical scriptures. Souls/spirits live forever and this is a scientific and biblical fact. Souls are energy, and energy never dies or dissipates; it just transfers somewhere else. Your pets are alive in the spirit dimension in their glorified bodies, and they are in God's dimension and on his frequency.

What is a soul? Let's define this word. According to Webster's dictionary it means, *"The principal of life, feeling, thought, and actions of a living entity." (p. 1253)* We all know that animals have these traits and qualities. Therefore we know that they have souls because they are living entities with life, feelings, thoughts, actions, and breath.

What is a spirit? Webster's defines a spirit as, *"A supernatural, incorporeal part of all living creatures. An individual as characterized by a particular attitude, character." (p. 1265)*

All animal lovers know that each animal has a different attitude, personality, and character. They also have feelings, thoughts, and actions. So therefore we know for a fact that animals have souls and spirits. Notice the definition above states, *all* living creatures.

Today, studies increasingly show that animals have feelings and emotions. Scientists have only recently studied animals for these attributes where before they were ignored. Parrots can become cranky and many animals can become terrified. Many animals get sad such as, monkeys, cats, and dogs. Many animals can get embarrassed. Elephants, dolphins, whales, and many other animals can express joy and they are also able to feel grief. And we know that household pets express all these emotions and feelings.

Experiments have shown that rats become upset when seeing surgery performed on other rats. They also display manners and exhibit caring for their fellow creatures. Experiments were performed and two rats were put in a cage together. They were given one piece of chocolate and one of the rats allowed the other rat to eat before it did. There's even evidence that rats like being tickled. *(Aeon)*

Charles Darwin stated that there was not much difference between humans and animals concerning feelings and emotions. And King Solomon said that we are no different or better than animals, as shown in the next verse. He said we are all on the same par.

> *"I said in mine heart concerning the estate of the sons of men, that God might manifest them, and that they might see that they themselves are beasts." (Ecclesiastes 3:18)*

King Solomon is saying that he wished God would show humans that they are beasts, and that we are no different than animals.

Animals are more aware of their feelings than humans because they are more cognizant of their existence and their environment, due to the fact that they have less problems to worry about than we do.

All creatures are sentient. According to Webster's the word sentient means, *"Having the power of perception by the senses. Characterized by sensation, feeling, and consciousness." (p. 1199)* And the word consciousness means, *"Aware of one's own existence. Having thoughts and feelings, full activity of the mind and senses and characterized by an entities own volition. To become aware of other's needs and one's own needs." (p. 284)*

There are many examples of animals showing concern for other animals and humans with disregard for their own well-being. This means that animals fit the description above as having a consciousness by being aware of their needs, your needs, and other animal's needs. There are countless true stories of animals who have saved the lives of humans and other animals, showing a consciousness of caring. The definition above says, to be "aware of other's needs." Which means animals can feel *empathy.* The capability of showing empathy alone shows that animals have souls. Webster's defines the word empathy as, *"The identification with or vicarious experiencing of the feelings, thoughts, etc. of another. The imaginative ascribing to an object of one's own feelings or attitudes." (p. 432)*

This means that one can feel or imagine how another is feeling and what they are thinking. You must have a soul to do this. Empathy is a spiritual feeling that comes from the soul. Every pet owner knows that when we feel pain or sorrow, our pets are able to empathize with us. Your animal can also feel empathy for you because your souls are bonded and this is a form of spiritual, or soul communication. Empathy is a *spiritual* action which emanates from the soul.

The Jewish culture refers to animals as *nephesh chayah* which literally means living soul. There are almost eighty scriptures in the bible that prove that animals do have souls/spirits, which I quote in my first and second books. God put his breath of life in all creatures and the word spirit translates as breath. When humans and animals die their spirits look just like they did in life, only younger and more vibrant and their souls shine with a white light. This is what I saw when I was in heaven. The soul is the core of all feelings, emotions, and desires. All creatures have these attributes.

Let's take an example of how God feels about his animals. We will see what God thinks of a horse. Remember, when Jesus comes back he will be riding a white horse and so will we.

"Hast thou given the horse strength? hast thou clothed his neck with thunder? Canst thou make him afraid as a grasshopper? the glory of his nostrils is terrible. He paweth in the valley, and rejoiceth in his strength: he goeth on to meet the armed men. He mocketh at fear, and is not affrighted; neither turneth he back from the sword." (Job 39:19-22)

You can see God is proud of his creation. He is actually bragging and telling Job that he is proud of his creation and that he loves his animals!

Animals and humans have the breath of life from God and with this breath comes not only life, but a soul and a spirit. The souls of animals are eternal just as ours are. Everything is eternal. The next verse verifies this.

"I know that, whatsoever God doeth, it shall be for ever." (Ecclesiastes 3:14)

Animals serve many purposes. They take care of the environment which ensures our existence and they

99

teach us spiritual values such as, unconditional love, unconditional forgiveness, and many other Godly and spiritual attributes. We animal lovers bond our soul with the soul of our animal. This is why we hurt so much when our beloved passes. We are suffering from spiritual pain, or soulful pain.

Animals teach us spiritual values such as unconditional love and forgiveness, which are spirits that emanate from the soul. God also uses his animals to accomplish his work the same as he uses humans. All creatures have a soul and spirit as seen in the following verse.

"In whose hand is the soul of
every living thing."
(Job 10:12)

In the preceding verse God tells us without reservation that animals do have souls and that he does take care of them here on earth, and in heaven too. God, the creator of all things is telling us that animals have souls. The verse states, "the soul of every living thing." Aren't animals alive? Yes they are, and they are in his hands.

The next scripture tells us that God created everything, and that he does save the souls of animals.

"Thou, even thou, art LORD alone; thou hast
made heaven, the heaven of heavens, with
all their host, the earth, and all things that
are therein, the seas, and all that is therein,
and thou preservest them all; and the host of
heaven worshippeth thee." (Nehemiah 9:6)

The last verse states that God preserves all things. Preserve means, *"To keep in existence. To protect from decay. To maintain possession of." (Merriam-Webster)* The verse also states, "the earth and all things that are therein." God is telling us that he saves every living creature on earth, which includes the animals. And if you notice, it says the host of heaven praises and worships God for doing this.

God took Enoch to heaven and showed him all the mysteries and secrets of heaven. While in heaven God told Enoch how deeply he loves his animals. To show how much God loves his animals he told Enoch that whomsoever defiles the soul of beasts, defiles his own soul. And that man will be judged on how he treats animals. He also told Enoch that the animals will be there in heaven standing beside Jesus to accuse all who mistreated them. God would not have told this to Enoch if animals weren't important to God. And it also proves that animals go to heaven because Enoch says that the animals will be standing next to Jesus in heaven on judgement day accusing the people that abused them. So we know that our animals will be in heaven waiting for us and they will greet us when we arrive. It will be a great day when we meet our beloved pets in heaven, but not so good for animal abusers.

Another verse below to prove that the souls of animals do go to heaven.

*"Then shall the dust return to the earth
as it was: and the spirit shall return unto
God who gave it." (Ecclesiastes 12:7)*

We now know that animals have souls/spirits and that they go to heaven because this verse tells us so. It says that the spirit returns to God in heaven. The earthly bodies of all creatures turn back to dust but the eternal soul returns to heaven to be with God. While in heaven God told me that everything comes back to him.

God loves us and he loves his animals as proven in the next verse.

*"Thou sendest forth thy spirit, they are
created; and thou renewest the face
of the earth. The Glory of the LORD
shall endure for ever: the LORD shall
rejoice in his works." (Psalm 104:31)*

This verse tells us that all creatures have a spirit (the spirit of God) and that God loves everything he created, including animals. The meaning of the word rejoice according to Webster's is, *"To feel joy or gladness; To take delight." (p. 1114)* God takes delight in all his creation and does not destroy anything that he loves. God loves every single creature that he created.

God really loves and cares about his animals, and they do have souls. And we know that God does allow us to see and communicate with them through signs, dreams, visions, and even spiritual manifestations.

The next verse tells us that God is love.

"He that loveth not, knoweth not God;
for God is love." (1 John 4:8)

This verse tells us that God is love and if you know God, then you know he is pure love. Our love for our pets is nowhere close to the awesome love of God. Think of how much you love your beloved animal. God's love is so vast and encompassing, that we cannot even begin to imagine it. Our ability to love is nothing compared to God's love. Do you really think that the awesome love of God would fail to save the spirits and souls of animals? God would never forget or neglect the soul of an innocent animal or deny us from communicating spiritually with our animals. Your beloved pet is in heaven and is receiving love that you cannot even comprehend.

Many people don't really think about this: Sheep are animals. Jesus calls us his sheep. He relates us to sheep.

"And this shall be a sign unto thee
from the LORD,
that the LORD will do this thing
that he hath spoken."
(Isaiah 38:7)

CHAPTER EIGHT

16 AFTERLIFE SIGNS FROM YOUR BELOVED PET

"What is a friend?
A single soul dwelling in two bodies."
-Aristotle

There are many various signs that our animals give us from the afterlife and there are also many ways that we can communicate with them into the afterlife. Many people state that they see, hear, smell, and also feel the presence of their beloved pet who has passed on. They have also reported seeing their pets in dreams, visions, NDE's, and spiritual manifestations. This chapter will help you to recognize and know the signs that your beloved pet may send to you in signs, dreams, visions, or spiritual visitations. And let's don't forget prophecy. Below are signs that our pets can send to us.

16 Signs From the Afterlife to Watch For:

1. A spiritual manifestation of your pet. Perhaps you see a fleeting image or shadow of your pet. Hearing your pet's paws or the clicking of toenails on the floor.

2. Hearing them drink from their water dish or any other noises they made while alive.

3. An object will have moved and you don't know how it moved, such as one of your pet's old toys.

4. Smells of your pet, or the smell of the food that you used to feed them.

5. A soft touch to your skin. Feeling something brush up against your leg or some other part of your body.

6. While lying in bed, you may feel something cuddle or lay down beside you and feel, or see a compression on the bed.

7. A sudden change in temperature in the room. It may become cooler or possibly warmer.

8. A cloud that is shaped like your pet that may remind you of your beloved pet while you were thinking of them, and you become happy and you *feel* it in your soul that it is a message from your pet.

9. A light or lamp may flicker while you are recalling a memory of your pet. Spirits are energy and their energy is electro-magnetic and therefore they affect electrical appliances and lights. Love is a spirit, but it is also energy. Praying releases

this energy so that your pet's spirit can use this energy to make contact and give you signs of their presence.

10. Butterflies and other insects are known to represent life and freedom. If you see butterflies, ladybugs, or crickets, it is your beloved pet telling you he or she is in heaven and is all right and free from death, and to stop worrying or feeling guilty.

11. Birds such as, hawks, robins, hummingbirds, blue jays, and cardinals are also signs from your beloved animal. If you see one of these birds while thinking of your beloved pet they are definite signs from your pet.

    Example: One day not long after my vision I was setting out back on my deck thinking of BJ and remembering how much I loved him and how unique he was. As I was sitting there a hummingbird flew right up to me. It was no more than six inches from my face. I stared at it and it stared at me. We stared at each other for a good five seconds and then it flew away. I knew it was a sign from BJ. He didn't want me to be sad and telling me that I had nothing to feel guilty about. Guilt is the number one emotion we feel after losing a pet.

12. If you see the number 444 frequently it means an animal spirit or an angel is watching over you, and that you should watch for a sign. Or it

could be the spirit of your beloved pet watching over you. It also means that you have a strong connection with God and that something special is about to happen. Perhaps a sign from your animal. Angels can also come in the form of animals.

13. A faint bark or meow. Hearing the jingle of your pet's collar or any other sound that your beloved pet made while alive.

14. Hearing a song or seeing a television show that triggers memories of your beloved pet while you were thinking of your pet.

15. Reading, seeing, or hearing something out of the blue that reminds you of your beloved animal while you are thinking or recalling a memory of your pet.

16. Whenever you see a rainbow, that is God telling you that your beloved pet is in heaven and alive forever. It is God's promise to all creatures. You must remember that all earthly bodies decay and die, but the spirit is energy and it lives forever.

A friend of mine was sent several signs. One was from a picture taken of a triple rainbow and the other was a sign from an animal.

Robert lost his beloved dog Blue Bear and he was devastated by the loss. He prayed for a sign to know that his beloved dog was safe and in heaven. One day as he arrived at the hospital where he worked it was raining. As he was parking his car the sun began breaking through the clouds. He entered the hospital and as he walked down the hall thinking of Blue Bear an employee that he knew stopped him in the hallway and told him to look out the window at the rainbow. When Robert looked out the big, glass window he saw a triple rainbow. He took a picture of it and when he looked at the picture he saw Blue Bear's face. Several people who were there saw Blue Bear's face too. One employee exclaimed, "it really is his face!" This was a sign from heaven that Blue Bear was at peace and alive in heaven.

Six months later he was given another sign. Robert was sad because it was Blue Bear's birthday and he wanted to wish him a happy birthday. He prayed and asked God to tell Blue Bear that he wished Blue Bear a happy birthday and then he prayed and asked God to give him a sign that God had told Blue Bear of his birthday wish. Robert told God that if he had heard him and did as he had asked, to send him a sign letting him know that God had relayed his happy birthday message to Blue Bear.

Robert asked for a sign that he knew would be nearly impossible for him to deny and if it happened, he would know it was real and from God. He told God to give him a definite sign which was to let him see a Husky that very day. Robert worked in a hospital and he knew that the chances of him seeing a Husky were slim next to none. And when he got off work it would be too dark to see a Husky, let alone any dog at that time of night.

Robert worked in the oncology department and when he arrived a co-worker approached him and told him that he needed to go down to room 608. Robert told him that he was too busy to go to the room and that he needed to get to work. His friend told him again that he had to go to the room. After refusing again, his friend insisted that he had to go. Finally, Robert went down to the end of the hall to the room and as he got near the door he heard the whining of a dog. When he entered the room he was in shock. There was a Husky that looked identical to Blue Bear.

The dog ran to Robert immediately and Robert began to pet the dog as tears welled up in his eyes. The dog belonged to the visitor of a cancer patient. Robert had worked there for thirty-one years and in that time he had never seen a dog on that floor, let alone a Husky that looked exactly like his dog and the dog ran to him as soon as he entered the room. Two beautiful signs from God telling Robert that his happy birthday wish to his beloved Blue Bear had been delivered and Blue Bear was in heaven and happy.

The messages that our pets send us no matter what form they are sent, are to let us know that they still love us and that they know that we love them. And also to let us know that they are doing just fine and that they are in the afterlife (heaven) waiting for us. They are also telling you not to feel guilty because they are in heaven and doing just fine. They are not just waiting for us to join them; they are expecting us!

There are some who do not believe in the afterlife or in signs from heaven. These are the same people who say that animals are, "just animals" and they more than likely don't believe in the afterlife, heaven, or God for that matter. If you receive one of these signs or have had this experience, the only thing that matters is that *you* know they are real.

"Your soul dreams those dreams;
not your body, not your mind.
Those dreams come true.
The soul travels all over the
world when you dream."
(Chippewa-John Thunderbird)

CHAPTER NINE

THE BELIEFS OF THE AMERICAN INDIAN ON DREAMS, VISIONS, SIGNS, AND SPIRITUAL VISITATIONS

"The soul would have no rainbow,
if the eye had no tears."
-Native American Proverb

Let's look for a moment at the beliefs of the Native American Indian concerning animal spirits, signs, visions, dreams, and spiritual visitations and how we animal lovers believe much of the same things.

The American Indian belief in animals and spirits is called Animism which is a belief based on spiritualism. They believed that everything has a spirit. They believed that an animal's spirit has supernatural powers and can convey messages from the spirit world and can even give one personal power. They also believed that spirit animals are guides for the human spirit and can appear in signs, dreams, visions, and spiritual manifestations, and that they can also protect a person. They also believed that they could learn from the earthly animals the same as we believe.

They believed that each human had a spirit animal that watched over them and protected them. And they also believed that the animals here on earth could teach them many spiritual lessons too. Don't animals teach us? Yes, they certainly do.

In most American Indian cultures they thought that animals were on an equal par with human beings. Animal lovers know and believe this too. Many tribes believed in a Great Spirit that created everything. So basically, they believed in God. And they considered Europeans to be thoughtless of nature and of the animals.

The American Indians knew how to tune into the frequency of God, or the Great Spirit. They would perform what is called a Vision Quest which also included dreams. They went on these quests to find out how to be a better person and for information about life itself by peering into the afterlife through dreams and visions. They would seek vision quests, dreams, and signs to improve their spiritual well-being and also their lives. Many of these vision quests involved spiritual animal manifestations that would give them vital information to live by. They believed that their spirits left their bodies and went through time and space (dimensions). These quests were to open up the spirit world and show them how to live according to the wishes of the Great Spirit. Don't we do this? Don't we pray and ask God to show us the right path. Many of us pray for signs, visions, and dreams too just as they did.

The American Indian knew that dreams, signs, visions, and animal (and human) spirit visitations were from the Great Spirit. They knew that these spiritual things were from God and they would seek these spiritual signs in order to live well. They were attuned to the spirit world and to God. They would fast in order to have a dream quest and many Christians fast too, in order to bring them closer to God when they pray and seek visions or in order to receive a word from God. Scientists have found that hunger changes a person's pathways in the brain and also changes the resonant frequency.

We animal lovers have many of the same beliefs as the American Indian when it concerns animals and their spirits. We know there is a spirit world and we know our animals are in the spirit dimension, or heaven. We know that animals have spirits and are loved by God. We crave to see our beloved pets and we also seek signs, dreams, and visions to see our pets. In a way, we too go on vision and dream quests to peer into the afterlife to see our beloved animals.

"Thou openest thy hand, and satisfiest the desire of every living thing."
(Psalm 145:16)

CHAPTER TEN

TRUE STORIES OF PEOPLE WHO RECEIVED SIGNS FROM THEIR PETS FROM THE AFTERLIFE

"Sometimes the truth must be experienced
...before one believes."
-Steven H. Woodward

Millions of people have received signs from the afterlife but sadly, not all post their stories on the internet so we really don't have an actual count but there are enough on the internet to know that these spiritual events do happen. And many of these stories can be verified. The following stories will help you to recognize any similar signs you may have experienced, or if they happen to you in the future you will know them for what they are.

The first story is about the spirit of a deceased dog

that connects spiritually with a living dog and a human. Mike inherited his mother's dog whose name was Gem and soon after Mike took Gem in, Gem passed on. In this story it seems as though Gem's spirit was a little upset that his favorite toy was in the paws of a new animal member of the family.

Gem had lived with Mike's mother most of his life but when Mike's mother passed away, Mike and his wife had to take Gem in. Several years later Gem passed of natural causes due to the fact that Gem was old at the time Mike and his wife had taken Gem into their home. Sometime later, Mike and his wife adopted a Yorkie that was two years old and they named him Yorkie. One day Mike was cleaning off the mantel and he saw one of Gem's toys on top of the mantel. The toy was a small, plastic Orca whale with a squeaker which happened to be Gem's favorite toy. It had been sitting there where Mike had placed it after Gem had passed.

He took the toy into the den and set it on the bookcase where he had placed all of Gem's other toys. He noticed Yorkie was following him spinning in circles and whining but Mike paid no attention to Yorkie and placed the toy on the bookshelf with the rest of Gem's toys, and then left the room.

After a little time, he heard Yorkie whining and jumping up and down in the room where he had placed the Orca toy. Mike went into the room to see what was going on with Yorkie and when he entered the room, Yorkie was in front of the mantel spinning in circles and whining. Yorkie was staring at the mantel where the toys were setting. He lifted Yorkie up eye level with the toys and Mike noticed that Yorkie's attention was fixed on the Orca toy. There were six toys on the mantel but when Yorkie saw the Orca he went crazy like he just had to have that one toy. Mike took the toy off the mantel and gave it to Yorkie. He then set Yorkie down on the floor with the toy and returned to the living room to watch TV. Minutes later Mike heard a loud banging above his head in the wall and he heard Yorkie in the kitchen growling and whining. Mike entered the kitchen and took the Orca toy away from Yorkie and noticed that Yorkie had chewed the tail off of the toy. Mike looked at the chewed off tail and then he took the toy over to the garbage can and dropped the toy and the tail into the trash can.

Once he placed the toy in the trash can the banging increased and got louder and yet there wasn't any wind or anything else that would have caused this noise. Finally, Mike went back into the kitchen and took the toy out of the trash can. He then took it into the other room placing it back on the bookshelf with the rest of Gem's toys. The banging stopped and has never happened again. The toy still sets on the mantel to this day. (YGS)

It seems as though Gem did not want Yorkie to play with his toy and he definitely sent a sign to let Mike know he did not like Yorkie playing with his toy.

This next story is about a dog's spirit that gave visual and physical signs. Mary's dog Yabba was almost seventeen when she died. Yabba survived cancer and several knee surgeries, but old age had finally taken her.

One morning Mary woke up and found that Yabba had

passed and of course Mary was devastated. Sometime later she decided to get her camera and began to call Yabba's name aloud. She then started taking pictures in different areas of the room. When she looked at the pictures she could see a faint picture of her dog Yabba.

This encouraged Mary and she began to talk to Yabba everyday hoping that Yabba might be able to hear her. One day Mary took out Yabba's ball, placed it on the floor and said, "Yabba, here's your ball. Come out and play." And to her amazement the ball rolled twice! When she squatted down she felt something brush up against her leg. Then she felt a tap on her arm. And she also heard the tap.

Later that night as she lay in her bed she felt a gentle bite on her toe. She said she could feel teeth on the top and bottom of her toe. Her instant reaction was to jerk her leg back and wonder what had happened. After several seconds she realized it was Yabba letting her know that she was there, and that she was okay. (YGS)

Mary had more than one sign from her beloved dog. She felt Yabba touch her, felt Yabba nibble on her toe, and Yabba's spirit moved the ball. And Mary also saw Yabba in several of the pictures that she had taken.

In this next story a cat's spirit seemed to be protecting his domain from the two living cats that still lived in the house. Beth owned three cats and one was a cat named Widget that had recently passed. Soon after her passing, Beth began to notice strange things happening that could not be explained.

One night around eleven p.m. Beth's sister came into her room and told her that the toy bin where they kept the cat's toys was shaking. Beth shrugged it off and went back to sleep. The following morning Beth noticed that some of the toys were out of the toy bin. Beth had two other cats and she knew that one of the cats never played with the toys and the other cat had slept in the bed with her sister that night as she did every night, and her sister always slept with the door closed. All the toys were in the bin when she and her sister had gone to bed that night.

She stated that one of the cats was always afraid to go downstairs to the basement where Widget used to hang out. Widget liked to lie at the foot of the stairs on the basement landing and the other cat would not go down there either after Widget's passing. Widget did not like one of the cats while alive and Beth believes that Widget was down there protecting her space from the other cats. Beth and the rest of the family have seen the basement door open on its own from time to time. She believes that Widget's spirit is still in the house and guarding her space. (YGS)

It seems as though Widget was still in the house. Perhaps she doesn't know she has passed and is still protecting her favorite space at the bottom of the steps.

Our next story is about a dog's spirit that manifested itself to its owner. She heard faint barking from a distance that sounded like her dog's barking. And then soon after, Betty saw the spirit of her dog run through the house.

On New Year's Eve Betty had to put Kahlua to sleep due to medical problems because she was suffering terribly. Three days later, early in the morning Betty heard Kahlua's distant bark. Betty heard her dog bark two more times and she became filled with grief and guilt because she had to put Kahlua to sleep.

Betty decided to sit down and write Kahlua a letter because she felt as though she had let Kahlua down. She typed the letter on her computer in Word Program and cried the entire time that she was typing the letter. As Betty got to the last line she typed, "I am sending this letter to heaven." Just as she finished the last line the document disappeared from the screen. She did not delete it nor did the program crash. She tried to find the letter that she had typed but it was lost somehow.

Several weeks later Betty and her husband were watching TV in the living room when a small black dog ran through the kitchen towards the bedroom. It was Kahlua! They both saw this manifestation which made them feel better knowing that Kahlua had come to tell them that she was fine and that Betty no longer needed to carry any guilt over Kahlua's passing. (YGS)

Perhaps Kahlua made the letter disappear to let Betty know that she did not need to apologize. She then manifested her spirit so that Betty and her husband would know that she was okay and that they did not have to worry about her, or feel guilty any longer. Spirits are energy and they can materialize here in this dimension using their energy and the energy of our love.

The following story is about a dog whose spirit energy stayed around for his owner to see him leave on his trip to rainbow bridge to join his master. The dog's name was Shandy. Peggy's husband had been the closest to Shandy but after her husband passed, Shandy was not himself.

Shandy was a Fox Terrier and he was her late husband's dog. After Peggy's husband passed away, Shandy began to mope around and seemed to lack energy and just wasn't as playful as he usually was. Peggy's late husband would take walks with Shandy and now Shandy was acting as though he had lost all interest in life. He didn't want to play and he would not eat.

Worried about Shandy, Peggy made an appointment with the veterinarian. After the doctor examined Shandy he found nothing wrong with Shandy physically so Peggy brought him back home. Later that night Peggy tried to feed him but Shandy still refused to eat. Peggy decided to sleep in the living room with Shandy close by to keep an eye on him. She woke up at about four a.m. to the sound of Shandy's whining and pawing at the front door. She got up quickly thinking Shandy needed to go out and relieve himself. She called to him saying, "Hold on Shandy, I'm coming!" She ran through the foyer thinking that Shandy was finally back to his old self.

Once she was in the hallway she could see Shandy at the front door wagging his tail and jumping up and down. Peggy suddenly realized she had to get her shoes before she could go outside. She ran back to her bedroom to get her shoes as she hollered back at Shandy that she would be right back. Upon entering the bedroom she glanced over at Shandy's bed, and there was Shandy! He was lying motionless. She went over and began to pet him and it was then that she realized he had passed during the night. Shandy could not have made it from the front door and down the hallway to the bedroom where his body laid without Peggy seeing him. When Peggy returned to the front door there was no Shandy. Peggy believes that it was Shandy's spirit telling her he was fine and he was going to join her husband in the afterlife. (YGS)

Shandy's spirit was telling Peggy that he was going to meet her husband in the afterlife and that they were both in heaven in their glorified bodies, and that they were both fine. Apparently, Shandy had grieved himself to death. Perhaps Peggy's deceased husband had come to get Shandy and had met Shandy's spirit at the door to take him into the afterlife.

I would like to add a thought about this story. Shandy was her husband's dog and you can see in this story that Shandy was depressed after the death of Peggy's husband. All animal lovers know that when another pet or family member passes, many times the animals that are in the family become depressed and grieve just as humans do.

The following story is about a Pomeranian dog named Angel. In this story Angel leaves a unique and undeniable sign for Janice.

Angel was eleven years old when she succumbed to cancer but passed peacefully, and with little pain. The veterinarian that Janice and Angel went to always made a paw impression for every client whose pet had passed on, and he would also put it on a keepsake. Janice realized she had never seen Angel's paw print and she studied the print cast and made a mental note of what it looked like. She said that she had never really given much thought to what Angel's paw prints looked like until she studied the print that the doctor had given her. In her mind she supposed that every dog had its own individual paw print.

Janice had Angel cremated and took her ashes to a beach in Florida where Angel used to love to walk. Janice spread Angel's ashes along the beach and when she returned home to Michigan, there had been a snowstorm and the new fallen snow had covered everything. She remembered thinking how pretty the new fallen snow looked as she walked to her apartment. Janice lived in a small apartment on the second level and on her level there were only two apartments; hers, and the second one which had been vacant for some time.

There was only one set of stairs that led to her upstairs apartment and as she got to the bottom of the stairs, she stopped and froze in place. There was a set of paw prints leading up the stairs but there were none coming down. The prints started at the bottom first step and went straight up to her door. She looked around and saw no other paw prints anywhere. She wondered how that was possible and after consideration, Janice decided that they had to be Angel's. She pulled out the paw print the Veterinarian had given her and compared it with the ones in the snow and they looked identical.

Janice smiled thinking, "Angel beat me back from Florida." And she knew that Angel was telling her that she was still around and doing well. (YGS)

This was a definite sign for Janice. Angel was telling Janice that she was gone, but not really gone. Her spirit was still around letting Janice know that she was alive in the spirit world.

Our next story is about a cat named Roo and how his spirit came in a dream to comfort his distraught owner whose name is Jim.

Jim had just recently moved to Boston and he was a bit anxious because he didn't like living in a big city. He clung closer to his cat Roo after they had moved which made him feel more comfortable. They had been together for a long time and he knew that his and Roo's spirits had bonded because he could look at Roo and know what he was thinking without Roo having to tell him with a meow, or a gentle nudge of the paw. Six months after moving to Boston, Roo passed.

Jim was heartbroken and his parents tried to console him but it didn't ease the pain any. Jim tried to move on, but Jim knew that Roo was that "special one" and it would be a fight to overcome his depression of losing his best friend. One night Jim was in bed and he was having a hard time dealing with the loss of Roo and he began to cry. He then felt a loving, warm cuddle on his cheek which caused him to sit straight up in bed. He then heard a soft meow and a low purring sound. He laid back down and he then felt a gentle rub against his shoulder that was soft like fur. Jim was not scared and in fact, he felt comforted. He then saw a shadow of a cat on the wall of his room. He knew it was Roo and that Roo was there with him. He went back to sleep and dreamed that Roo was sleeping in the bed with him. He dreamed that Roo kissed him and when he woke up he felt his cheek, and it was wet. (YGS)

Jim was given several signs that night which were auditory, visual, and a physical manifestation in the form of a shadow. Jim knew what these signs meant and he also knew who it was, and it gave him closure on the passing of his beloved Roo.

This next story is about a dream visitation from a Pit Bull named Tauri and a sign from an insect from beyond. Pam noticed that her Pit Bull whose name was Tuck, seemed lonely. She decided to adopt another dog so Tuck would have a friend.

Tuck was three years old and he seemed despondent. Pam thought about getting Tuck a friend but then she thought of all the trouble that comes with a new puppy and all the aggravation that is involved such as, training, cleaning up after it, bathing, etc. she was a bit hesitant about adopting a puppy. She thought of Tuck and how lonely he seemed, but she was still undecided.

Pam's husband had a cousin who had acquired a female Pit Bull puppy from a friend of his whose dog had recently had a litter, but not long after his cousin and his wife adopted the puppy they were thinking of getting rid of it. Pam thought about adopting the puppy, but then decided not to. After about a month Pam's husband told her that his cousin was ready to give up the dog and wanted to know if Pam had decided whether she wanted the dog or not. Finally, Pam had come to a decision and told her husband that if his cousin were ready to give up the dog she would take her.

Pam and her husband went to his cousin's house to pick up Tauri and there was a crowd of people there as they had a big family. Pam was behind the crowd of people and Tauri ran through the crowd of people and straight to Pam. Tauri had blue/green eyes and gray velvet fur and Pam fell in love instantly. The cousin's wife did not want to give Tauri up and Pam's heart sank because she had fallen in love at first sight. But his cousin's wife finally gave in and gave the dog to Pam. They told Pam that the dog's name was Tauri. Pam took the dog home and the family took to Tauri instantly and she fit right in. Tuck seemed to be happier than he had been in a long time.

Not long after this, Tauri became sick with parvo virus and she passed quickly as there was nothing the doctor could do for her. It was devastating for the whole family, including Tuck. That night Pam laid down and was crying with many emotions running through her mind and spirit. Finally, Pam called to Tauri and told her that she was always welcome in this house for love and kisses.

Pam's son had gotten the closest to Tauri. He had become closer than anyone in the family. The night Tauri passed, Pam's son had a visitation in a dream from Tauri. He said that in his dream he was crying and Tauri pushed the bedroom door open as she had learned to do when alive. Tauri then ran and jumped up on the bed with her son. Tauri and her son began to give each other kisses and then Tauri curled up beside him and went to sleep. He then woke up from his dream and felt his face where Tauri had licked him and his face was wet.

The next day, the family was sitting on the front porch

looking at pictures and videos of Tauri and reminiscing bitter-sweet memories of Tauri. Pam happened to look over at the spot where Tauri would play in the water and there was a little baby butterfly. The butterfly remained there until the family finally went inside the house thirty minutes later. Pam knew her son's dream was real and that the butterfly was a conformation of the dream. Tauri had come back to let the family know she was in heaven and doing simply fine. (YGS)

Tauri had definitely given the family a sign. She gave them two signs: one in a dream and another by a butterfly. I also believe that Tauri sent Tuck a message too, telling Tuck that she was fine.

This story is about an animal that God sent to save another animal. I saved the best story for last. This dog was an angel in the form of an animal.

A couple named John and Tony had a dog named Sailor and they had gotten him as a puppy at five weeks old. They had him for over ten years. He was John's best friend and John and his wife loved Sailor like a child. Sailor would ride with John in the truck wherever John went with his head resting on John's knee. One day as they pulled into the driveway Sailor jumped out of the passenger side as he always did, but this time was different.

When Sailor jumped out of the truck he hit the ground with a yelp and he laid there in the driveway and would not get up. Sailor was paralyzed and they didn't know why, or what had happened. They took Sailor to the veterinarian immediately and the doctor told them that Sailor was damaged internally and there was nothing that the doctor could do for him. The doctor then said he would put Sailor to sleep but John and Tony said no. They wanted to keep him to see if he would recover although they knew he probably wouldn't, but they just couldn't put Sailor down at that time. They decided to give Sailor a couple of days to see if he would heal because the thought of putting him down at that time was too much, so they took him home.

They took Sailor home and made him comfortable in a bed they made for him on the bedroom floor. They brought him food and water but Sailor refused to eat or drink. Sailor laid there for two days and his condition only worsened. On the second day John told his wife that Sailor was in a lot of pain and they decided that tomorrow morning they would take him back to the doctor and have him put to sleep because it was hurting them to watch Sailor suffer. Tony told John that she was going to say a prayer and ask God to please send an angel to heal him. She went to her bedroom and prayed and prayed. But sadly, Sailor was not getting any better.

It was killing John and Tony to see Sailor in this condition, and knowing they would have to put him to sleep in the morning made them even more miserable. They were terribly upset and crying for their beloved Sailor, and praying that God would send a miracle.

Through tears John told Sailor, "Well, I guess this is it my friend." He took off Sailor's collar and took it to the garage where he kept the collars from two other dogs he had previously owned before Sailor, and he hung the collar up with the others.

The following morning John got up early before they

took Sailor to the doctor's office. As he walked out the front door and began to walk down the driveway he saw a little brown dog coming up the driveway towards him. It was a female dog and she looked lost and she wasn't wearing a collar. He thought perhaps she was a stray. John thought she looked hungry so he took the dog into the house to give her some food and water. But she would not eat or drink and then she began to walk around inside the house. She walked into the bedroom where Sailor was lying and she sat down in front of Sailor and stared at him. After about a minute she went up to Sailor and nudged her nose against Sailor's neck. Immediately after the stray dog nudged him, Sailor slowly got up and staggering a little bit, and shaking somewhat, he began to walk to the bedroom door. After a minute or so Sailor began to walk around wagging his tale with the stray dog behind him. Sailor had regained his health and was fine. John called Tony and when she saw Sailor walking around alive and well, she was totally surprised. She told John that God had answered her prayers and had sent an angel in the form of a dog. But that is not the end of this story.

They did not know where the stray dog had come from and thought that maybe it was lost and that someone might be looking for it. John called the local radio station and reported the lost dog thinking that maybe someone would come and claim the dog. A few hours later the owner of the dog called John on the phone and said she would be over to get her dog. Her name was Karen and she told John and Tony that she had just moved to the neighborhood recently and had come from Georgia, and that she lived *three or four miles from John's house. The dog had run off without her collar and had not come back. There were several miles of wooded area between Karen's house and John and Tony's house and the dog did not know the area, and Karen was afraid her dog had gotten lost.*

After Karen arrived she pulled out the dog's collar from her bag and put it on the dog. After Karen had put the collar on the dog John looked at the collar and read the name on the collar. The collar said Angel. The dog's name was Angel! Tony and John knew that God had sent an angel in the form of a dog to save Sailor. God had given Angel the power to heal. (It's A Miracle TV & YouTube.)

God had sent a dog named Angel to cure Sailor. Angel had traveled four or five miles through a wooded area that was unknown to her and went straight to John's house. She went into the bedroom where Sailor was and touched him and he was cured. They believe that God sent an angel in the form of a dog to answer John and Tony's prayers.

A Manifestation of God Himself. This is a true story that happened to a friend of mine. It is not about animals but the spirit has pushed me to include it in this book because it shows that God does answer prayers, and that he still performs miracles for anyone who asks. His name is Troy and we worked together for sixteen years.

For the sixteen years that I worked with Troy, many of those years he constantly suffered from severe back pain. He wore lift belts every day and also medical pads that delivered heat, and he had also missed some time at work due to his back.

I had told him about my vision of BJ a few years before this and he respected me and did not make fun of me, but I knew he doubted my story of the vision I had of BJ. We worked night shift and one evening he called in sick because his back pain was so horrible that he couldn't get out of the bed, nor was he able to walk. Later, about six-thirty in the evening he called me. He was crying and said he didn't know who else to call because he said that I was the only one who would believe what had happened to him that afternoon.

He told me that he had been lying on the floor in extreme pain and was praying like he had never prayed before. He begged God to please take the pain away or just go ahead and take him now. He related to me that he suddenly saw God, and that God began to work on his back. He said that he could see God taking strange, nasty black things out of his back and also taking muscles and ligaments out and replacing them. He was on the floor for almost an hour. When God had finished, Troy said he felt like he had a new back and there was no more pain. He just laid there for a while because he was scared to try and get up, but finally he got up and was surprised to find that he had no pain whatsoever in his back. He was in shock and disbelief at what had just happened.

Two years has passed since this divine event and still to this day, Troy has no back pain. He does not wear a back brace or require any more pain medication or heating pads. I told him that it made me feel good knowing that he also had a divine experience. Now I had someone who not only believed me, but had experienced a divine intervention too. We both had a divine experience and it was like he and I had a secret that no one else was aware of, or believed. However, it is hard not to believe this story if you had seen how bad his back hurt and all the medical aides he had to use. Some co-workers that knew Troy, knew something strange had happened to heal his back. And due to this, some of them believed the miracle really happened. But of course, there were some that didn't believe. Like I said, you may not believe it until it happens to you!

Miracles, prophecies, healings, signs, visions, dreams, and spiritual visitations are real. We have the *power* to see and communicate with our beloved pets who have passed. But we must use prayer. God is all-powerful and he can do whatever he wants. Only seek these things in prayer with Jesus. Again, anything else can be dangerous.

*"And the ass said unto Ba'laam, Am
not I thine ass, upon which
thou hast ridden ever since I
was thine unto this day?
was I ever wont to do so unto thee?
And he said, Nay." (Numbers 22:30)*

CHAPTER ELEVEN

DO ANIMALS HAVE AN INTERNAL DIALOGUE?

Do animals have an inner dialogue? This is a question that has been debated for quite some time. Many scientists and psychologists believe that they do, and some believe that they don't. Charles Darwin and many philosophers believed that animals do have an internal dialogue, but not on our level. I believe that they do because they must have some type of internal dialogue in order to think, reason, play, plan ahead, remember, and function. This would mean that they have an *inner voice* which would require some type of an internal language. In one of my books I have proven that animals can plan ahead, play, and perform many other reasoning abilities just as humans do, and this requires some type of an inner language. Many animals dream which also requires some type of inner thought/

dialogue. And there have been tests that have proven that animals do have an internal dialogue. However, we animal lovers already know this by watching and observing our precious animals.

Some believe that the internal dialogue of animals only consists of pictures and/or symbols. If they do use symbols or pictures in their internal dialogue, then these symbols and pictures must have names/labels. *All* creatures must label any symbols or pictures in their mind in order to understand and differentiate between each picture or symbol that they are seeing in their mind. By teaching our pets our own words we have added to their inner dialogue. Just because an animal cannot verbally talk to us does not in any way negate the fact that they have an inner dialogue. We know that animals can communicate with us and they also communicate with other animals. We also know that all creatures have a spirit. And all creatures with a spirit have an inner voice, which comes from the spirit.

Let's examine the facts which are mostly common sense which many animal lovers know just by observation. First, try to look at something without using any words. It's impossible! If I look at the clock on the wall I must describe it to myself in order to know and understand what I am looking at. And if I *picture* a clock in my mind I must describe it to myself in order to understand what I am thinking about. In other words, I must label these pictures/symbols. We humans must use some type of inner dialogue in order to think, reason, and identify what we are looking at.

Animals must do the same or they would be confused and could not function in the world. If they had no internal dialogue they would be completely stupid and dysfunctional. It is obvious that animals do have an internal dialogue if one only observes. There is really no need for tests as some scientists, psychologists, etc. have performed in order to prove or disprove whether animals have an internal dialogue.

I will use my dog Jasper as an example. Of course this will apply to most animals. I have taught Jasper words such as sit, lie down, bone, treat, mommy, daddy, and a few other words. If I speak any of these words he knows what I mean. Jasper likes to play a game I call fetch. Only I am the one who fetches. He will take a treat or dog bone out with him when he goes to the bathroom. He will drop it somewhere in the yard. And when he is ready to go back inside he will stand and stare at me with a look that says, "get my bone for me," or "be a good boy and fetch the bone Steven." I will have to search the yard and retrieve the bone where he has left it and give it to him, and then he is happy and we go back into the house. But sometimes I will refuse to get it and I tell him to get his bone which he does. He knows exactly where in the yard he left it and we have a big yard with many trees and bushes. This also shows that he has the ability to remember, which entails having an internal dialogue.

Another example. If I want to play with him I will tell him to get a certain toy that I will call by name. One such toy is a stuffed skunk. We have told him that this toy is called skunky. If I tell him to get skunky he will go dig into his toy box which has about thirty toys in it, and he will bring back the stuffed skunk. If I tell Jasper that Lauren and Nickie are coming today his ears will go erect and his body will stiffen and he will run to the window and look for the grandkids. This is absolute proof that he has an internal dialogue and a *memory*. He knows the words/names of the grandchildren and responds by looking out the window to the driveway to see if they are outside. If you notice, he not only looks for them but he also looks for their car in the driveway. He knows what a car is and what it looks like. And he also knows that cars are in driveways. His internal dialogue and memory tell him that they will arrive in a car outside in the driveway. This also proves that an animal's inner dialogue is able to make connections between objects or events in the present and from the *past*. We know that animals have memories and without an internal dialogue, memories are not possible. And one fact is certain; internal dialogue never stops.

In the bible God tells us that he allowed Balaam's donkey to speak to him. (Numbers 22:30) This tells us that God gave the donkey the ability to speak long enough to scold his owner. And the donkey knew exactly what to say. But most importantly it tells us that the animal had an internal dialogue along with a memory, the same as we have. The donkey told Balaam that he had been loyal to Balaam since birth, so why would he stop now? This would require a memory.

Animals have their own vocal language, be it a

growl, bark, meow, etc. We may not understand their meaning, but they do. And they also learn some of our vocal language, or our words that we teach them. Think about this. People around the world have pets. Let's say a person in Spain has a dog and speaks to it in Spanish. The animal will learn these Spanish words and commands. Now let's say that this dog is brought to America and an American adopts the animal and begins to teach it English words and commands. The animal will then learn English words and commands and will respond to these words. So basically, some animals can be bi-lingual. How many people do you know that are bi-lingual? Not many!

We know from previous books that I have written that animals have souls and that they can think, reason, play, plan ahead, feel emotions, etc. My point being is that animals *do have* an inner dialogue or they would not be able to think, reason, plan ahead, or function at all. We also know that animals have memories and without an inner dialogue, memories are not possible. Memories and inner dialogue are an attribute of the spirit and we know that all animals have spirits. Memories and inner dialogue go hand in hand. You can't have one without the other.

*"And all flesh shall
see the salvation of God."
(Luke 3:6)*

AN ANIMAL SPIRITUAL POEM FOR PET LOSS

-From The Book,
"Healing Prayers and Meditations For Pet Loss."
By Steven H. Woodward

"Last Night"

Last night I lay in my bed,
With dreams of you in my head,
I woke up with a start,
To a room empty and dark.

I thought I heard the jingle of your collar chain,
Which I thought was rather strange.
And then I thought I heard your paws upon the floor,
And a familiar whine at my door.

I thought I heard the squeak of your toy,
And for a moment, my heart was filled with joy.
Could it be that your spirit came to visit me?
To let me know that you are happy and free.

Did I hear you drink from your water dish?
Is this a dream? Or perhaps only a wish?
Then I saw your spirit at my bedroom door,
And I knew that you were alive for evermore.

Then you turned and looked at me,
Because you knew that I could see.
Your spirit had come to let me know,
You were alive and safe, and I could let you go.

Then I heard you whisper softly in my ear,
The love we shared will always keep me near,
And all the love inside our heart,
Can never, ever keep us apart.

-Steven H. Woodward

"The LORD is good to all:
and his tender mercies are over all his works."
(Psalm 145:9)

HOW TO DEFEND THE POINT THAT ANIMALS HAVE SPIRITS AND GO TO HEAVEN WITH TWO SIMPLE QUESTIONS

The next time someone tells you that animals don't have souls/spirits and don't go to heaven especially if they profess to be a Christian or a minister, ask them this:

> *You:* "Do you believe animals have souls and go to heaven?"
>
> *Them:* "No, it doesn't say that in the bible" or "I don't know."
>
> *You:* "Doesn't the bible say that the love of God is unlimited?"
>
> *Them:* "Yes, it certainly does."
>
> *You:* "So, if you say that animals don't have souls/ spirits and don't go to heaven, then aren't you limiting the love of God?"
>
> Usually this shuts them up but they might say:
>
> *Them:* "The bible speaks of dogs in a negative way."

You: "Yes because the Jewish culture believed that dogs were the dirtiest, lowest animals alive, so God was speaking to them on their level so they would understand what he was telling them. God spoke to them using their cultural level of beliefs to make them understand his message. The Jewish culture considered all gentiles to be dogs and that's what they called all gentiles. The Jews considered all non-Jews or people who did not know God as "dogs." Remember, at one time only the Jews knew of the one true God. When God states in the bible that he would throw them into the outer darkness with the dogs he was actually saying that he would cast them into hell with the other non-believers, or gentiles. Or basically, the un-washed.

You can also quote them the verses from this book and also from my other books which contain almost eighty scriptures that prove animals have souls and do go to heaven.

"I have received more love and understanding from animals than from some of my own family members. And I have seen animals who act like people, and people who act like animals."
-Steven H. Woodward

STRANGE FACTS ABOUT ANIMALS

* Butterflies taste things with their feet.
* A Penguin called a Gentoo Penguin proposes with a pebble.
* Horses and cats cannot withstand a black widow bite, but the bite does not bother sheep, rabbits, and dogs.
* Polar bears are left-handed. Or if you prefer, left-pawed.
* Seahorses take only one mate in a lifetime.
* There is only one animal in the world where the male becomes pregnant. The Seahorse.
* The tongue of a Blue whale weighs more than an elephant.
* Clownfish are all born as a male and can change their sex.
* When bats leave their cave they always turn left.
* Sea otters always hold hands when they sleep.

* Dolphins sleep with one eye open and half their brain is asleep, while the other half of their brain is awake.
* There is a lizard in the amazon called the "Jesus Christ Lizard" because it can run across, and on top of the water.
* Cows, dogs, cats, elephants, and many other animals can suffer separation anxiety.
* A cat's nose pad is like a human fingerprint; no two are alike.
* There were three dogs that actually survived the sinking of the Titanic.
* A worm has five hearts.
* A giant Clam picks a rock to live on and never moves from this chosen place until it dies.
* A breed of dog called a Basenji does not bark, but it can yodel.
* A polar bear's fur is not white. The hair is actually colorless. The strands of its fur are hollow, and the hair reflects light. Their skin is black, which soaks up the warm sunlight and keeps them warm and cozy.
* An ostrich's legs are so powerful that they can kill a man or a lion.
* Anteaters can eat as much as 35,000 ants in a single day.

(Global Animal)

EPILOUGE

I pray this book has convinced you that there is a spirit world and that it is possible to communicate with our beloved pets in the afterlife through Jesus Christ. And if you already know that these things are real, I pray that you go through God in this endeavor. If you are not a believer in God and have lost a beloved animal friend I urge you to try praying to God for a vision, sign, dream, or even a spiritual visitation. Just give it a try. You have nothing to lose. God bless you. If you would like to get close to God I have put the Sinner's prayer below. You only need to speak it aloud.

S.H.W.

The Sinners Prayer

Dear God, I know that I (your name) am a sinner and now I ask you to please forgive me of all my sins. I believe in my heart that Jesus is your son; that he died for me on the cross and that you raised him back to life.

Jesus, I declare that you are my Lord and Savior and I open my heart to you. Wash me clean of all my sins with the precious blood of Jesus Christ and come into my heart and change me and help me to follow you all the days of my life. Please help me to be more like you and to do your will. In the name of Jesus Christ I pray. Amen.

ABOUT THE AUTHOR

Steven Woodward was born in Houston Texas and has lived in several states in the south but now resides in West Virginia with his wife, two sons, and four grandchildren and his dog Jasper. He enjoys hobbies such as playing guitar, banjo, and harmonica.

Steven spent four years in the United States Navy as a Communications Technician and was Honor Man of his boot camp company and he also served as an Educational Petty officer.

Steven graduated from Shepherd University in 2001 with a Psychology degree; graduating with full honors and was inducted into two Psychology Honor Societies and won two Scholarships, graduating Magna Cum Laude. Steven published two pieces of literature in the Shepherd University annual literature book entitled, "Sans Merci" at Shepherd University. Steven has published seven books for pet loss, proof animals go to heaven, and animal abuse awareness.

Steven has been a music teacher and swimming instructor. Steven has also worked as an Educator/

Trainer for Federal Service where he instructed work in computers, JACHO, TQI, QA, and many other subjects for Federal employees.

Steven has worked as a psychologist/counselor in the field of substance abuse and family counseling and has now dedicated his life to helping people with pet loss grief and proving that animals have souls, and that they do go to heaven through his books.

Steven and Marie have a Cairn Terrier named Jasper.

BOOKS BY STEVEN H. WOODWARD

BOOKS FOR PET LOSS AND PROOF OF THE AFTERLIFE FOR ANIMALS

"Biblical Proof Animals Do Go To Heaven" By Steven H. Woodward (2012)

When Steven lost his beloved dog BJ he was devastated. Steven had to know if BJ was in heaven or just a pile of dust. After praying for three weeks Steven was given a vision where he was taken to heaven to see BJ and his other two dogs Petey and Duke. Read of his vision and all the proof that he was given that proves that animals have souls and do go to heaven! A book for pet loss. No matter what animal you have owned. An Amazon best seller. Book/Kindle/Nook/Itunes/Google Books/Audible.

"God's Revelations Of Animals And People" By Steven H. Woodward (2017)

Seven years after writing his first book, Steven was given many more revelations of proof that animals do go to heaven. This is the second book in the "Biblical Proof" series. His second book contains much more amazing proof and he also includes some of his personal visions. Steven also answers questions that people have asked him about his first book regarding what he saw in heaven. Questions such as, *"What did your dogs look like in heaven?"* *"Will my pet be raptured?"* *"Will I see my beloved animal in heaven?"* Also in this book, Steven dispels several myths about the bible, and reveals several secrets of the bible. Steven's books will help you better understand the bible. *Also included are the amazing secrets of the animals that were given to Enoch while he was in heaven.* A book for pet loss. No matter what pet you have owned. Book/Kindle/Nook/Itunes/Google Books.

"BJ: A Dog's Journey Into The Afterlife" By Steven H. Woodward (2018)

Based on true divine events! This is a beautiful endearing story of the afterlife, redemption, and forgiveness for one man and one dog. A story of one dog's search for love and a home, and one man's only hope to learn about forgiveness. Unconditional love will take one man and a stray dog to a place they could never imagine. A story of fiction based on *true divine events*. BJ (the dog) narrates this heart-felt story.

BJ has a near-death experience and goes to heaven but he is sent back on a mission. He tries to negotiate with God to stay, but he must come back to earth and save a man he has never met. BJ is streetwise and he doesn't care much for humans, but he is determined to complete his mission. This story is about BJ's comical and dramatic journey to find this mystery man and unconditional love, and all the strange people he encounters on his journey to find this mystery man.

A great book that helps people to understand how animals think and feel, which is much like us. A book that teaches young children how precious animals really are. A book for all ages and a great book for pet loss. No matter what type of animal you have lost. Book/Kindle/Nook/Itunes/Google Books.

"How To Recover From The Heartbreak Of Pet Loss"
By Steven H. Woodward (2019)

A book of healing words, advice, prayers, and great healing tools. Contains both *Scientific and Biblical proof* that our beloved pets have souls and do go to heaven and why we shouldn't grieve or feel guilty upon the death of our beloved pet. This book explores the facts and proofs of the afterlife, the soul, and heaven for animals. Steven shows how much science and the bible agree on these very subjects.

Steven also shares secrets and revelations about the animals that he was given while in heaven. Find out what really causes the pain of pet loss and why you should feel no guilt. Learn the secrets of why, and how animal lovers bond their souls with the souls of animals. Plus, a Ten-Step guide to help you through the difficult times. Also included, *Amazing True stories of people who have had NDE's and have seen their animals in heaven, and True stories of animals that have saved humans*. A book for pet loss. No matter what type of animal you have lost. Book/Kindle/Nook/Itunes/Google Books.

"How To Have Visions And Supernatural Knowledge In The Bible You Didn't Know Existed" By Steven H. Woodward. (2020)

Get ready for a journey into the afterlife through Dreams and Visions! Learn how to see and communicate with your beloved pets in the Afterlife. Learn the *supernatural secrets* and mysteries of God's animals, and the bible.

Learn how to win the argument when people try to say animals don't go to heaven. Debunk their narrative and give them the proof that will change their minds! Learn the secrets of how and why we are able to bond with our furry friends.

This book contains a detailed guide on how to have *Dreams and Visions* in order to contact and see your beloved pet. Do our beloved animals communicate with us after they have passed? The answer is yes! Do you want to see and communicate with your beloved pet that has passed? Do you want to know if your pet is in heaven? A guide for peering into the afterlife.

Plus, Steven explains many other mysteries of the

bible. Learn about the secret Gospel of "Q" that has recently been found. Find out the divine frequencies and the divine numbers and how they affect us, and what they mean. Steven explains who and what the Watchers, Aliens, Demons, Giants, and the Nephilim are, and why we need to know these facts. Find out what is going on at the CERN and what they are doing, and many other hidden mysteries that are happening now that are being intentionally hidden from us.

Many Christians wonder if they are truly Saved. This book will show you if you are truly Saved or not. Are you ready for the End of the Age? This book will let you know what to look for and the hidden things that they don't want you to know! Book/Kindle/Nook/Itunes/Google Books.

"Healing Prayers And Meditations For Pet Loss" by Steven H. Woodward (2021)

From the Author of the Amazon Best Seller, "Biblical Proof Animals do go to Heaven." A daily devotional for pet loss. A book for healing and peace and medicine for the soul. Pet loss is real and it is a life-changing event for many of us. We feel dark and empty from our loss and we feel as though life has lost its meaning. We have feelings of needless guilt and deep sorrow, and we tend to isolate ourselves. Our pain is a spiritual pain.

We animal lovers bond with the spirit of our animals through our unconditional love. These are gifts that many do not have. Our pets are family members and we become distraught on their passing. Many of us feel the loss of a pet much more than the death of a friend or family member, and we wonder why. Many people do not understand our grief from losing a beloved pet and we are left on our own to deal with this tragic loss. This book contains valuable healing *Tools, Advise, Spiritual facts, and Prayers* to help you through the loss of a beloved pet. This book answers many questions you have about pet loss and its after-effects; how to cope with pet loss and all the emotions and feelings that come with the loss of a pet. Included are thirteen Spiritual Healing Poems for pet loss grief in the last section of the book by Steven and Marie. This book also gives proof that animals do go to heaven. Book/Kindle/Nook/Itunes/Google Books.

A BOOK BY MARIE WOODWARD

"Jasper The Dog Who Knew Too Much" a book of fiction by Steven's wife Marie Woodward. (2020)

A story of romance, comedy, drama, mystery, divine dreams, a miracle, and a determined dog named Jasper. Ellie lives in Breezewood and has been through a nasty divorce after her husband ran off with another woman, and now she has sworn off men. She swears she will never be with another man as long as she lives. Ellie has strange dreams about her dog Belle who has recently passed and struggles to understand their meaning.

Johnathan has lost his family and his dog while

serving in Iraq. Wounded in action, he ends up in the VA hospital in the small town of Breezewood where Ellie lives and he decides to stay. Johnathan rents a house just behind Ellie which neither of them is aware of. When he and Ellie first meet in town they despise one another. She hates men and he thinks she's crazy.

By chance, they must save a drowning dog together and they name him Jasper. After arguing, they decide to share the dog as in a child custody case, agreeing to share him on alternating weeks. Things get hilarious and out of control as they argue over who should keep Jasper, and who knows best for him.

Are animals smarter than humans? Jasper thinks they are! Jasper has plans of his own for these two humans. Sometimes it takes an animal to show humans how to love. A story of fiction with a surprising twist, an awesome miracle, and a great ending. If you believe in miracles you will love this tale. A book for pet loss. Book/Kindle/Nook/Itunes/Google Books/And now on Audible.

Visit Steven Woodward's Facebook Page at:
Steven Woodward or visit this link:
www.facebook.com/profile.php?id=100010267894532
Visit Steven's website at http://www.stevenhwoodward.com
Steven Woodward's books can be purchased at Xulon publishing, amazon.com or barnesandnoble.com and many other web sites. All books available in Book and Kindle and two now on Audible.

REFERENCES USED

*© Aeon Media Group Ltd. 2012-2022. Do only humans have souls, or do animals have them too? Aeon Ideas.

*Christian Headlines By Veronica Neffinger. April 21, 2017 - Lions Reportedly Save Pastor and His Friends from Attack by Islamic Extremists – Christian News Headlines (christianheadlines.com) Copyright 2022. Christian Headlines.com.

*FreqE 1.com. What is 963Hz Frequency? | Why is it useful? | Your connection to the Divine, also known as Christ Consciousness which is Unconditional Love. By Alan Drobnak. (freqe1.com.) C. 2021.

*Ghost Stories in Category: Pets/Animals - Page 1 - Your Ghost Stories (YGS). Copyright 2006-2022.

*Global Animal Weird Animal Facts: Fun Facts About Animals | Copyright 2022. Global animals foundation. A non-profit 501©(3).

*Godencounters.com/james-w-goll-bio/https://goden counters.com/james-w-goll-bio/

*Guideposts. https://www.guideposts.org/inspiration/ miracles/12-types-of-heaven-sent-visions by Kaylin Kaupish. Copywrite 2022.

*How Do Dogs Hear So Well? - Petful by Dr. Pippa Elliot. Copyright - June 4, 2019. scienceline.ucsb.edu/ getkey.php?key=596 frequencies dog can see and hear - Search (bing.com)

*Indierockcafe. making patterns with sand and frequencies - Search (bing.com) 07/05/2021. Indie Rock Café. Copywrite 2007-2022.

*It's a Miracle TV. April 6, 2016. Youtube. Sailor's Angel. Soldiers' Angel.com. Copyright 2022.

*King James Bible, Holman Bible Publishers; Copyright 1998. Mass market edition

005405430.

*Merriam-Webster Prophet Definition & Meaning - Merriam-Webster Copyright 2022.

Merriam-Webster, Incorporated. 2022.

*NDE/Near death-experiences and the afterlife. Quantum Theory Supports Near-Death Experiences - Near-Death

Experiences and the Afterlife. By Kevin Williams. Sept. 21, 2019. NDE/Copyright 2022.

* Random House Webster's College Dictionary. Copyright 2000 by Random House, Inc. April 2000 Second Revised.

*Solbu.net Did NASA really prove the Bible accounts of Joshua and Hezekiah that a day is missing? – Johnny A. Solbu. www.solbu.net. Written by Johnny A. Solbu. Copywrite-Feb. 28, 2017. Christian Issues website.

*The Om Shoppe. Feb. 13.2017 by the OM Shopee. Copyright 2022. Does Love Have a Frequency?

Printed in the United States
by Baker & Taylor Publisher Services